THE
POWER
OF
LIGHT

WILSON SANTOS

The Power of Light
by Wilson Santos

ISBN: 978-1-942991-19-9

Published by
Editorial RENUEVO

Contents

Introduction

Words are like a lifesaver, that when someone is drowning you through it out to him and the person has the opportunity to grab on to it, or drown. When we enter into dimensions where there is no life, that kingdom is of death. There are many dimensions that lack life and many people enter there many times without realizing it, bringing upon themselves and their loved ones destruction to their future generations— generations in darkness and without purpose, that should have life. Everything turns to darkness when hope dies. Desperation is an internal emptiness of light. When there is light, discouragement disappears because this is part of the darkness of conscience. The conscience can be elevated to another dimension and the original state recovered.

It's impossible for people to see light when they enter into a state of darkness. It's impossible to restore for a better life, those who have fallen once. Those who have the promise and embrace it can sit in high places; in those places ordinary men can't reach you or destroy you. As the song says,

"Fly high, fly high.
Don't be a seagull in the sea.
People shoot to kill
When we fly too low."

In high places, we are not only free from envy, spells, incantations, evil looks, and evil witchcraft. We are also free from being a victim of wrongs, evil, and from the challenges and the problems that we witness and face in this world.

To wake up means "to know the truth." And this truth is part of a world of light and illumination. Religions, politics, educational centers, and earthly systems are made to keep people in a world of immense darkness. Few people want you to be free, and you should know who they are, just like you need to identify those who want to keep you in ignorance. It's easy to enslave the ignorant. This is the why the powers of this world are united against the Truth, because "the truth sets you free". Only those who bring their conscience to that Truth can escape the trap, come out of ignorance, and ascend to heavenly places. These people are the only one who can save the world of all the negative energy, and all the evil influences.

Without knowledge, I can't live, without understanding,

I don't exist, and without love, I am nothing. I just think I do. This knowledge transcends any knowledge that anyone can obtain in an educational center; it's the secret that the great men of history have used. Frequency is elevated by the power of the mind and the power of man begins in his thoughts. To elevate the frequency of the thoughts we have to think about what is pure, what is good, what is necessary, and whatever has a good name. We have to be holy and humble of heart. Everything comes from a source: we begin there and to that we are going. People don't need the answer for everything; they only need to enter into the source to acquire the knowledge of the Great "I AM". He will tell you where you came from, where you are going, and who you really are, because the Great "I AM" lives within you.

Man was born with perfect thoughts, but they became contaminated, causing him to stop living in the world of faith, to live in the world of reason. "Reasoning is used by he who cannot believe." When I say this phrase, many people say to me, "Wilson, isn't reasoning what scientists use to venture into science?" No, they think that is reasoning, but in reality, it's faith. As persons who think, we have to use reasoning, but after using faith. This is the only way to get to unknown places and to the unknown world. Whoever made the first scientific advance, whatever that was, had to believe that the unseen was going to become visible.

A person who loses order, also loses the purpose of things. The Eternal put everything in order, because this order gives the universe the power to self-create and evolve. The same principle applies to you, and to everything that is under your control. The control of man starts within him, with his thoughts. Thoughts are under our absolute control.

Light is everywhere, and its principal manifestation is love. When love is lost, the meaning of life is lost, and with this, the ability to dream. We were born for greatness, to shine. No life is more important than another, and only throughout time we can see the great purpose. Don't put down the little one that is next to you; he is a being loaded with Light and purpose. Purpose is individual, is unique. Give time to the individual that is next to you, encourage him, teach him, and show him his potential. Soon you will see his Light shine.

I spent a lot of time thinking whether or not to publish this book. The concepts expressed here are not very common, though similar concepts can be seen here and there. I am one of those people who believe that nothing is new. I believe that everything comes from a source. I think that knowledge is simply hidden, and it is our duty to go out and look for it.

A good example is, those who look for minerals. They search in places where it seems that there is nothing.

Once, I met a man who would go to the riverbanks to search for gold. To me, gold can only be found in mines, but not in rivers. The historical account of the Spanish Conquest tells of the natives collecting gold from the rivers. When Christopher Columbus came to America, the native Americans were using gold. To them, gold was of no more value than any other metal. In fact, the Spaniards soon realized how ignorant they were as to the value of gold and began to exchange mirrors for this precious metal.

Knowledge is the starting point of every man and every woman in preparation for life. People have many dreams and desires, but die without seeing them come true. And though some don't accomplish their dreams for lack of action, lack of tenacity or a desire to work, others don't see their dreams fulfilled for a lack of knowledge. Whoever starts a company and fails, probably did so due to a lack of proper training. Man is not a failure, he is ignorant, and the only power against ignorance is knowledge. No one can accomplishes anything if he doesn't have the knowledge to do so. The power of Light lies in the fact that everything that is touched by knowledge is under Truth, and that Truth will set you free.

The Beginning is Light

The origin of the universe, and the origin of humanity has been expressed in differing postulations, which have come to be a part of human beliefs, but none can be proven in a laboratory. In this chapter I am going to mention two of the best known, the theory of the BIG BANG, and the claim of CREATIONISTS.

The first claims that everything began with an explosion the size of a grain of rice. Explosion of what? It could not have been from any matter because there was only energy and no matter. It couldn't have been a star because stars didn't exist. At that point there was only energy, and we know that energy comes from Light. The theory states that protons exploded and in so doing, produced a singular light. According to this explanation, something happened in the darkness that gave place to a singular explosion and that kept growing until it created millions of galaxies, planets, solar systems and stars. There is a certain truth is this theory: light did expand into space creating an immense universe. The theory of the BIG BANG states that everything was together and disorderly, but when the explosion happened, light radiated and so began the expansion of the universe as we know it, and who knows, maybe of another that we don't know about.

Everything came from empty space, or rather, from an unknown dimension. The scientist, Albert Einstein, was the first person who recognized that what we call 'empty space', is not 'the absence of anything' but rather, what we don't understand. Cosmologist Edward Kold said: "95% of reality is invisible." Even knowing this, many people who only talk about evolution, and deny any truth about a Superior Being, brand faith as an instrument for ignorant people.

Yet, all the things we see and use, originated in someone's faith. If 95% of what exists in the universe cannot be seen, this means that even those who negate the existence of a Creator, are sustained by the power of faith, because without faith, they couldn't continue with their beliefs and experiments. This leads me to say that there is a Light of faith in anything that has been discovered and created. It is a primary power that makes possible all the other laws of the universe. Light is hope. It is faith, power, joy, acceptance, transformation, strength, and power that takes us to purpose. It's about that power that I will be talking about, and about how this Light that gave origin to everything that exists, continues to be the center of everything.

Light – The Origin of Everything That Exists

The story of creation says, "In the beginning God created the heavens and the earth. Now the earth was formless and empty, darkness was over the surface of the deep, and the Spirit of God was hovering over the waters. And God said, 'Let there be the light,' and there was light." The Big Bang Theory, talks about an origin that started more than three hundred billion years ago, while the account written by Moses begins by saying, "In the beginning God created the heavens and the earth. Now the earth was formless and empty..."

Imagine that you are reading the quote mentioned above as a long and continuous text, exactly the same as it was written by Moses—that is to say, without the numeration of verses as we know it—and that the intention of the author was not exactly give a perfect order, but instead, to tells us the story exactly how it happened. Then, the author should have said, "At the beginning, thousands of millions of years ago, God created the heavens and the earth. Before that, everything was messy, empty and there was no expansion, no light, only darkness. Then God, who was the only being that existed before Creation said, 'Let there be light.'" Scientists say that, as light expands, so does the universe. I believe that in Genesis, there is a revelation of two beginnings: the beginning of the earth and the beginning of Adam and Eve, in a period of time of 9 to 10 thousand years; and a beginning that started thousands of millions of years ago. You may say, "Wilson, where do you get that information?" First, I get it from the logic of creation and science, because those of us, who believe in creation, believe that God had no beginning or end. And, that He existed before everything else, and that He was the one who designed everything that exists. Thus, we cannot be closed-minded and believe that a God who has no beginning nor end started a creation 9 to 10 thousand of years ago.

Second, to believe that a vast universe was created together with this tiny planet is too radical. If God is so powerful, as we believe He is, why would He spend an eternity doing nothing? Or wait for the moment to create this world? The third argument I have about God's creation is: a God that is so big, with a vast universe, would not create only one livable planet. There are many more worlds. This is only one of them. I believe that Creation keeps extending in the infinite universe, and that will never stop. This doesn't contradict anyone's faith, but it does contradict the traditions of many. One of the major problems of people who call themselves believers is that they live with traditions. They want to ignore reality, and the laws that God designed together with the existence of the universe.

We see that even Jesus suffered as a result of the power of traditions. Religious people of that time were the ones who deified their traditions and killed Him.

For over 1500 years, anyone who tried to bring light to the existence of humanity was killed, accused of heresy and demonized, but history shows that most of these people, who died, were right. These massacres affected all kinds of knowledge. We see that even Jesus suffered as a result of the power of traditions. Religious people of that time were the ones who deified their traditions and killed Him. This scourge of ignorance and religious traditions, gave rise to the phrase quoted by Karl Marx in 1844, "Religion is the opium of the people." This quote appears on Marx's publication, "Contribution to the Critique of Hegel's Philosophy and Right", and used by other philosophers.

About Creation, the difference between the scientific arguments and faith is that science sees everything through the lens of the laboratory; they talk about particles and matter, and those create and develop slowly. We see everything through the lens of faith. We believe that every particle, every planet, every living thing, matter, energy and substance has its origin in the God that doesn't have end. "He said it, and it was created. He ordered and it came to existence."

To me, both stories, the Creation and the Big Bang Theory are similar. The difference between one and the other is that one theory is being formulated by a man who lived three thousand five hundred ago, and his only goal was to give us knowledge about the existence of humanity. His science was divine revelation, which he passed on to his generations. The other theory is based on modern men and the science that seeks to explain humanity itself.

I have my beliefs about revelation, which I respect and have faith in. However, I cannot stop believing in science because both are God's revelations. The God who revealed the Bible is the same that revealed science, because all knowledge comes from Him "By Him...and for Him." My point here is, in regards to the story that you decide to believe, we have to accept that both theories began by saying that everything that exists originated with the expansion of Light.

Revelation and Science

Knowledge is the beginning of all science. It is possible that Moses could have proven his hypothesis if he had his own laboratory. That is why I say that revelation is the beginning of science, because knowledge does not belong to us.

All knowledge is a supernatural revelation from a Master Mind that oversees everything. Everything that is taken to a laboratory is born from a hypothesis and most hypotheses comes from the mind of the Eternal.

What is a hypothesis? It is the thought of someone about something hidden that could be a reality. There is no hypothesis without revelation, because the hypothesis is the formulation of a theory that is only believed by he who accepts it and believes it in his being. It is only true to he who believes and will never be proven without the help of many experiments in a laboratory.

The Big Bang Theory is just a theory and it has not been proven in a laboratory. The Creation concept is similar in that, in order to accept either of the two, you need to believe and what is surprising to me is that both begin speaking about Light.

The second reason why I say that in every theory there is a revelation and that there is a relationship between the two postulations in question, is that both say that Light gave origin to everything. Light is the beginning of everything and it allows men to continue living. Those who know that they are sons of Light don't speak as one who has no direction, but understand that they have the power to make changes in this world. "I am the light of the world. Whoever follows me will never walk in darkness, but will have the light of life." This thought points to the identity of a person who is aware of who he is, and understands what his identity can mean for others.

A Theory is a Light

Some time ago, I was standing in front of my window, crying tears of sorrow for having lost everything, and being left bankrupt. I expected at any moment that an office would knock the door down, taking everything, leaving my family in the street. While I was crying and observing the sleet of a cold winter fall, a Light shone inside me and said, "So why don't you begin writing a book, but one that gives hope to people! A book that talks about the goodness of God. This could change your situation."

Immediately I thought, to whom am I going to sell it? When I allowed that negative thought to come into my mind, darkness invaded and covered me to the point that I wanted to reject the Light. Every time a negative thought comes to your mind, you are being dragged into the darkness.

> *Every time a negative thought comes to your mind, you are being dragged into the darkness.*

I reacted by eliminating that negative thought and returning to reflect on the Light. I aligned my thinking within my inner being and I said to myself, "Why not? After all, I have nothing to lose, and everything to win."

Immediately I started to write, and from that thought, my

first book originated which turned out to be a total success in sales. When the thought of writing a book came to my mind, it was only an idea, but became a reality when I allowed faith to take action, in other words, I believed.

Nothing begins with the creation of a fortune, an object or an invention. Everything is born from an idea that becomes a theory, and every theory needs faith in order to be proven, but there will never be faith unless there is vision.

Light Will Always Have Power Over Darkness

A lady approached me while I was giving a series of lectures in Utah, in the United States. She told me she was three days from divorcing her husband, but after listening to the lectures she decided to stop the process of divorce.

Why did I start this section with this story? Because it illustrates what I want to teach: that Light has power over everything. Later in the book I will talk about the topic of Words, but for now you need to know that these are also Light.

When this lady listened to my words of hope and

encouragement, she started to believe in something that she thought was dead. How did this happen? The truth is that everything can be rebuilt when you believe. Faith is a source of illumination.

Contrary to what the world in which we live tells you, this is the truth that will take you to a higher level. Culture and the media that directly influences us, together with the religious spirit, have taught us that everything in life comes with a lot of effort, pain, and hard work.

However, this is not true. God left everything within our reach and when the first man was on this earth, and didn't lack anything and they didn't have to worry about anything. All they had to do was keep close to the Infinite Source, who was represented by the "Tree of Life". This was the fount of eternal life.

Eternal life has always been the master plan for man. The Creator of everything did not want man to lack for anything, and his plan was that man lack nothing and that he live for eternity. This was the science of life, but man opted for another science: The Science of Good and Evil.

If you analyze it, you will see that the science of light

comes first (as a unity), and parallel, there is the science of good and evil. By choosing the science of good and evil, Man chose light and darkness, life and death, wealth and poverty, health and sickness. This was in the natural (the tree), but in the spiritual (the science): life or death, faith or fear, courage or cowardice, loyalty or disloyalty, restlessness or peace. Today all of these are choices, but the Eternal One always made it that way, with the difference that the first couple was born in a crib of gold and chose to live in the mire.

In the beginning, the choice was the mire and not the gold; but now the choice is the gold, because we are born in 'the mire'. In the beginning, God made everything to be good. This is His heart and this is a beginning that will take us to a different existence. Knowing that we were created to live in the Light, and that this Light is the origin of everything that is good, gives us power over the darkness.

The Light Shines

A friend told me about an experience he had on one of his trips. This is his story:

I travelled one weekend to Oregon, in the United States, to give a series of seminars. When I got off the plane and

Chapter 1

I was going to get my suitcases, I saw a girl that observed me with curiosity.

At first, I pretended I didn't notice her, but moments later she approached me and asked, "What do you do for living? I see you are well dressed, and that's not very common, you know. Are you a politician or something like that?"

"No," I answered. "I am a motivator and speaker."

"Ah, that smells like something religious," she answered.

"Do you have a problem with religious people?"

"Yes," she continued, "they are hypocrites and judge people in a very ugly way."

I knew that unfortunately, this girl was not far from the truth. People who call themselves religious tend to judge people in an inhumane way, and although I know that it is not good to generalize, I also know that when people have a negative opinion of a belief, country, race or political party, they are bleeding from some personal wound or they are living in some type of ignorance.

I looked squarely at her and said,

Although my faith is Christian, I do not consider myself religious, nor do I like to judge others.

That's what they all say, but if I told you what I do for a living, you would change your opinion.

What do you do? I asked.

I am a prostitute, that is what I do.

As for what you do, I have no right to judge you, I said.

To that she replied, Are you just saying that to make me feel good or to simply try to prove your theory that you don't judge people? But if you truly are the type of person who you say you are, let me ask you this question: Would you sleep with me?

No, I replied.

See, she said, you consider me inferior to you and of bad life. That is the simple truth and there is no other way to see it.

I paused for a moment while I observed her carefully, then I replied,

The fact that I would not go to a room in a hotel to have sex with you does not mean that I consider you inferior, quite the contrary; I see you as someone greater than you consider yourself. I know that you don't do what you do for sport or because it is the only way for you to make an income, rather, because you have no idea that you can have something much better. There are many things to sell, and it doesn't have to be your body. If you only knew who you were, then you would not sell yourself to anybody.

And who am I? she asked, looking at me with daring eyes.

Someone who is capable of being happy in the moment that she decides; able to live a better life and make positive changes. A person full of light, with eternal and better purposes for living. A queen, created only to reign.

She shook her head a bit surprised and said,

When I was young and stupid I believed those fairy tales, that I would find a good man, that I would study, graduate and have a great career; that I would marry in a gorgeous white dress and my children would take the same path. That was until I saw reality—that the world is cruel and that life is not easy, that the ideal man would never appear. Quite the contrary, my first romantic experience with a man was with someone who would not take "No!" for an answer, and like a savage beast ripped my clothes off leaving me in great pain and a black cloud in my chest that seems like will never be erased.

That was when I woke up from my silly dream and faced the reality of life—that the world is for a certain few; where the poor will always be poor and always abused. Nobody does justice for us, and no one cares about us. Take me for example, not even my parents cared about me. The truth is that all that motivation that you preach neither any other theory of personal improvement can change that fact. There are more sad people than happy; more unjust than just; more greedy than generous.

My dear reader, the truth is that the world is full of people like this girl, that don't comprehend their value. People who let the bitter things of life ruin them and keep them from seeing the Light. I don't know what

> *To be aware that we are people who come from the Light, gives us power against all the things that are in the darkness.*

you are going through at this time in your life, neither what will happen to you tomorrow, but I can assure you that tomorrow's level of living will be much higher if today you see the Light.

This woman could offer her body, but my friend could offer her something better—the Light of hope, true love, and the secret to obtain forgiveness. That is the difference. When you understand who you are and know what you possess, you will not let your life become something inferior to what you are. My friend let his Light shine to the girl, and he made her understand that his feeling towards her was not rejection, but rather acceptance and value. Those of us who dedicate our time to leadership, will never be able to help people by rejecting and judging them.

Many times people who consider themselves to be right, confuse the world because they consider others who practice certain things o have certain ideas as people who are wrong, rather than notice the qualities they possess.

To be aware that we are people who come from the Light, gives us power against all the things that are in the darkness. This is my point when I talk about my friend and the young lady he met in Oregon. She approached him as a butterfly that chooses to be close to the light. This young lady, like a disoriented butterfly, was looking for the Light. That was obvious, because the place was full of people, but my friend caught her eyes and she didn't know why. He didn't know. He didn't need to condemn her or tell her that her way of living wasn't good, neither did he need to explain to her that there is a place of torment prepared for people like herself; he limited himself to give what he had—words of hope, confidence, greatness, power, mercy, and especially, of change.

The account of Creation details how God said: "Let there be the light," and there was light. God called the light "day," and the darkness he called "night." And there was evening, and there was morning – the first day. Where a light is lit, darkness disappears; no matter how dense it is, Light will have power over darkness.

Finally, my friend said, "The conversation with this young lady lasted another half hour. We talked and laughed while we were waiting. At the end, she gave me a hug, dried her tears and said, 'Thank you, this has been my best day in many years. I never thought someone could make me feel so happy in a healthy way.' I started walking away, and as I left she added, 'Ah… and you are right… yours is better than mine.'"

She wasn't better because my friend had a theory of how

the universe works, or who are those who go to God's paradise, but because he gave her a sense of identity, because in her dark brain, a Light was turned on, and it shone. Now, as for how long will it will continue to shine, that will be up to her.

The conclusion of what I say here is that those who accept the Big Bang Theory, like those of us who accept the Creation Theory, have a truth that unites us, "Light shone in the darkness and Light gave origin to all things that exist." That truth is absolute, and I don't see the reason why science and faith fight. I think that science without faith is dead, and faith without science is also dead. James himself, one of the closest men to the Master, Jesus Christ, said it like this, "Faith without works is dead." Science is based on work, but also on faith. Why? Because every hypothesis and every theory is based on faith. Because that is what faith is, the confidence that even if something cannot be seen at the moment, we are confidant that it exists.

This was the beginning of that all that exists that has come to us: the telephone, the airplane, medicine, electricity, space travel, etc. Everything came through men and women who saw and believed in things that had never been proven, or things never seen; but they saw it in their visions and dreams and they believed in them. Every man who goes after the Light, will believe in things that no one accepts as true, and he will be extraordinary, because Light is always on the rise, and a man who knows about this power will never stagnate.

Chapter 2

The Expansion of
Consciousness

Some theories about Light state that it is gradually expanding in the universe, conquering and invading space. You may say, "How do you know that?" It is easy to say because of the scientific investigations as well as the affirmation of the Bible, which is the book that talks about the creation of the lineage of Adam and Eve.

Science says that the universe has been extending itself for 13.85 billion years. I understand that when we are talking about Creation, science has a problem because they measure the age of the universe by quantum science and they base their studies on fragments of meteors discovered and the speed of light travel. But none of this is exact because man does not have all of the answers to these matters.

On the other hand, if we talk about an infinite God, then I don't see any contradiction between the scientific theory that the world is millions of years old and the theory of the creation of man. What I mean to say is that the universe, whether we understand it or not, has been extending itself for billions of years. And this we can prove.

> *The only reason is that everything was expanding for millions of years, until light came to our planet earth.*

The other theory regarding the creation of the universe is the "Creationist Theory" and I am going to base my point of view on this proposition for the rest of this chapter.

The Bible says that, "The earth was without form and void, and darkness was on the face of the deep." (Genesis 1:2) It is important to note that this account is not talking about the creation of the entire universe, but rather exclusively this planet. What is clear is that the account says that before the order of everything, there was a planet (earth) surrounded in darkness; a planet that existed for millions of years, but without light, and therefore, without life. If the Almighty is infinite and in the beginning he created the heavens and the earth, it means that the beginning of the universe was not the beginning of the existence of the earth, because it is of common knowledge that the universe is older than our planet earth. Why?

1.- Because the existence of man on earth, theologically speaking, is no more than six to ten thousand years.

2.- Because the universe is too enormous for this planet the only one that has inhabitants.

3.- And another even more important reason: What was an Infinite Being with unlimited time on his hands, who in the beginning created everything, waiting for all eternity to create a small planet like this one? The only reason is that everything was expanding for millions of years, until light came to our planet earth.

The Perfect Model

God finished creating everything on the earth He finally created man. "So God created man to His own image, in the image of God He create him; male and female

He created them… and he said to them, 'Be fruitful and increase in number, fill the earth and subdue it…' Now the Lord had planted a garden in the east of Eden, and there He put the man He had formed."

There are mysteries here and few Bible readers pay attention to it.

1.- The man that God created was not put in all of the earth but rather in a special place called Eden, comparable to an embassy today (but brought from heaven), and place this couple in a specific place on earth as ambassadors and told them, "Your mission is to extend this Kingdom of Light to the whole earth."

2.- Why and whom did they have to dominate, if they were alone, and man in the original plan was not created to be governed but to govern?

3.- What were they to fill the earth with? Other humans? Or something else? If you observe chapter 5 of Genesis carefully, you will realize that outside of the garden of Eden everything was not so perfect and good as inside the garden. Outside, there was still darkness and that was the place to be subdued by the man living in the garden, which was full of light.

The account says that on the first day of creation, light was made and on the third day lights were created in the solar system to light up the day and night on earth. What I understand in this is that the light mentioned on the first day y something more than the lights mentioned on the third day, such as the sun, the moon, and the stars.

That light represents the origin of everything. That light represents the beginning of everything created. It is a force that where it touches, consciousness of existence begins to exist. Only where there is consciousness of existence is there light. There can be a planet with water and animals, but if there is not a conscious mind, a mind that can perceive the universe and connect with the Master Mind, there will only be darkness and desolation. The power of the conscience, of life, and everything that there is in the universe is what makes of man a creation connected with Light. Outside of this force everything is darkness. Man's power lies in knowing who he is, where he comes from and what he does.

Ignorance makes men opaque and dull. The following is a clear example, when an animal is well trained, many become confused, thinking that he is an animal that can think and is aware of his mental state. But the animal does not have a mind. You could look him in the eyes and think that he has the same thoughts that you do, but the truth is that the animal doesn't think, he does not know that he exists and that he coexists with man in a universe so immense and beautiful. A universe so huge that experts say its geographical extension is 93 million light years across. Animals don't look for the light, because they are not aware of it. If only animal and planets existed, there would no be real existence. The existence of everything has its place in the creation of man, and only man gives honor to his Creator because they are connected to one another.

What I will say next, will sound a little bit hard to understand, but is necessary that you understand it: "The universe exists because man exists." Descartes said, *"Cogito ergo sum"*, ("I think, therefore I am"). Although it is believed that this is the idea that gave origin to evolution, it also gives power to the Creation. Without the awareness of the things that exist, there is no creation. Evolution, when it doesn't leave the Creator, out of the picture, is real because everything has evolved and keeps evolving. Man should evolve because he was created with the purpose to give existence to all; even to God; because he was created "in the image and likeness of God."

That was the purpose of Eden then, to fill with Light

every place that was in darkness (which is the same as making all of creation aware of existence). The first thing that existed was the Light, or a Mastermind (God); then, a similar mind (the man); and with this, darkness started to disappear in all of the abyss.

I used to sit and watch the movie, "The Walking Dead". I don't know exactly why I liked it, because the drama itself was about people who died and came back from the dead to eat other people.

People who are dead, those who have lost their dream, have the capacity to kill others who are still living.

But the person who came back from the dead didn't have a sense of who he was, neither did he have a sense of what was happening around him. He would just see some other person that was alive and eat them, even if it was his son or his mother.

I take advantage of this narrative to make an application. People who are dead, those who have lost their dream, have the capacity to kill others who are still living. In the movie the dead ate their father, mother, sister, children; for them, they were all the same. The dead would eat meat, but they didn't do it with a level of consciousness or purpose.

This movie goes well with the topic of this chapter. Only the levels of awareness make people live or die, or make things exist or not exist. In the movie, if someone's daughter died, she would come back as a zombie. That is the reason why the father did not bring her home, or feed her, despite how cruel it might have seemed. He destroyed her. He knew that even if she was walking and seemed to be alive, she was actually dead.

"The walking dead" could be good qualification to given to those who don't have a state of consciousness, for all those who don't know they exist, or acknowledge their present state, or they are not living up to the purpose for which they were created. In fact, people who are alive, but seem to be dead, those whose dreams have faded away, they are capable of killing others who are living their life to the fullest. When the Light comes to a mind, the mind becomes reasonable. When the Light of existence comes to a planet, the planet becomes alive and conscious, and this consciousness creates a human being with a creative mind.

The Parable of the Prodigal Son tells of a rich man who had two sons. "The youngest one told his father, 'Father, give me the part of the inheritance that is mine,' and the father divided the property and gave him his part. Not too long after that, getting all his money, the son went away to far away country..."

In the minds of many people, inheritance is something that is passed on to the children when the parents die. In reality, the inheritance is with the father and belongs to the child as soon as it is born. But we have forgotten that, because the conscious man does not want to admit that away from the father, he will not be able to live the marvelous quality of life that his father offers him.

In this parable, the father gave his son the inheritance portion that corresponded to him, and the son went and wasted it in an immoral fashion. People who see riches and possessions as a trampoline to life a licentious life, and they use it to humiliate, abuse, destroy, even their own life, because they are in a state of unconsciousness and lack of purpose.

The story continues describing how that when the son had squandered all his inheritance with women, pleasure and vice, he ended up feeding pigs and reached a point of hunger that he was willing to eat the pig food. Note that he doesn't realize that what he is doing is not natural and keeping company with swine is not an appropriate place for a human being to live. No man was created to live on the level of an animal. But there are many who prefer that life style.

Every time a girl is sexually abused by her father; every time a man takes the life of another man; or those who destroy their life using toxic substances, every time we feel hatred or fail to help others, every time we use inequality as an excuse to promote racism, or shame our family with our mindset of defeat or scarcity, we are living below the level of the life of pigs.

Then we read, "He longed to fill his stomach with the pods that the pigs were eating, but no one gave him anything. When he came to his senses, he said, 'How many of my father's hired men have food to spare, and here I am starving to death.'"

"When he came to his senses," shows the power that we have to retake our purpose; the power that we have to make changes and live the life that the Creator prepared for us to live.

The prodigal son came to his senses and said, "I will set out and go back to my father, and I will say to him, 'Father, I have sinned against heaven and against you. I am no longer worthy to be called your son, make me like one of your hired men.' So he got up and went to his father…"

I met a lady who had traveled to Dominican Republic to be in one of my leadership conferences. She said to me that her life was in a horrible darkness after her father's death. Her father was a good, hardworking man, but the way he died was not the most desirable, not even for a worst enemy. She said that while her father was working, some thieves came to his company; they tortured and chopped him up, killing him in a horrible manner. Since that day, a deep sadness overwhelmed her. She lived in an indecipherable darkness. She cried every day. She didn't even have a desire to eat. And she had lost the love of all those around her. She didn't even care about her seven children. She would only complain to God that He had been unfair to allow such cruelty.

One night, she couldn't sleep, and could not bear so much internal pain. She started talking to God. She asked Him to reveal her why that had happened to her father. Again, she told God about how good and hardworking her father had been. She insisted that bad people were allowed to be in this earth; why these bad people had not died instead of her father. Her father had been a good man. He hadn't hurt anybody.

While she was in that struggle, a voice came to her inner being and said to her, "Nothing occurs without a purpose." At that moment she came to her senses and said to herself, "Maybe my father, for whom I cry so much, and for whom I suffer, is in a better place."

Since that day, she had peace. That burden and that pain left her. This state of conscience is what I call "Light." It is the power to leave a state of inferior mentality to become aware that the universe belongs to us. All the things that come to our life, whether or not we understand it, are for our growth. It is this understanding which will help us to live an extraordinary life.

Like the woman, the young wealthy guy came to his senses. A Light came to him; a state of identity overwhelmed him. It was at that moment that he realized where he had allowed himself to get, and that such life didn't belong to him. Riches, comfort and happiness were at his father's side. That is why he was able to reach the decision to return to his father's house. However, first he had to acknowledge his wrong by telling himself, "I will set out and go back to my father, and I will say to him, 'Father, I have sinned against heaven and against you. I am no longer worthy to be called your son, make me like one of your hired men.'" When a person understands his identity, he prefers the home and inheritance of his father, above anything else.

Many people, when they are in a state of 'no conscience', abuse everything they touch, and wither everything that is put in their hands: their marriage, their finances, their health, their friends, and they think that the world around them is against them. They work hard and struggle daily trying to stay afloat, but instead, they sink more and more in a pig sty that doesn't offer them anything but a life of mediocrity.

> *When a person understands his identity, he prefers the home and inheritance of his father, above anything else.*

In that state of struggle, work and deterioration, they choose not to believe anyone; they choose to believe that God doesn't love them, and that He has forgotten them. Using the excuse that on this planet there is no enough resources for the overpopulation that already exists, they take their own lives in order to end their pain.

Others, when they are cornered by setbacks and trapped in their mistakes, they settle for thinking and believing that they were born for that: to survive and to live a life of scarcity that they will never be able to overcome. Men who lack identity survive, but struggle a lot. They believe that to do what they want, they only have what they own. As a result of that, they fall into deception, lies and extreme sacrifices, but they are unhappy, and so are those around them. Why? Because they believe that the world in covered with darkness, and there is nothing they can do to change it. They think that is too difficult to obtain good things, and the only thing they have left is to think that they lost the opportunity to grow, confining themselves to live with the pigs, accepting that these pigs will be their companions for life.

Do you want to get away from suffering? Don't forget that the answer lies in one thing: in the understanding that you have a Father; a Father that loves you dearly; a Father that is full of light; a Father who has made you the heir of a supernatural realm, where things have been given in abundance. But above all that, a Father who has his arms open, waiting for you to reach a 'state of consciousness' about who you are, what is your place, what is your kingdom, and your purpose on this planet. This is this way that you leave this dark world that enslaves you, and you go into the Light.

The parable tells us that when the prodigal son returned,

his father dressed him in new clothes and put a ring on his hand. He received him with honor, like a king. When you are living in the arms of the Light, you cannot live otherwise. Living like a king is your destiny, but the key is not hard work and struggle, neither the stinginess of those who save everything to have savings for the future, forgetting about the present. It is instead, to know that you deserve it because you have an inheritance. It is the power to receive something that was already prepared for you. It is the power to be still, letting the Light to create a new man in you. A man full of knowledge and wisdom, filled with power and greatness, one like the Father, who is full of power, energy, wisdom and light.

The Light That Enlightens Every Man

I was brought up in a religious environment where I was taught that God was only for those who were good, did not eat certain things and they strictly followed a certain way of living; that God had certain special people to whom he had given a type of manual, that they had to follow, believe and teach to those who would like to know the Light, and live in it. This is the lie of all oppressive religions.

One of the disciples of the Master Jesus Christ said,

"The true light, the one that gives light to any human being, was coming to this world." The Light of God does not manifest itself through a man or some religious institution; the Light of God is manifested through the "perfect man", through whom He restored the relationship between God and men. Once the relationship was restored, it is now available to all men. This is not easy to accept, however, and even though I am a Christian, I understand that the Light of God is not available for just Christians; it works around the world through the work of the Spirit.

The Light was given at the beginning, and was restored through the Son. "But when the Spirit of Truth comes, he will guide us into all truth…and you will not need anyone to teach you." For every man who doesn't want to walk in the darkness, there is an inner Light that guides him. That Light is the only truth; it cannot be sold, it cannot be kidnapped, and it doesn't belong to any group in particular. It is from the Creator and He gave it to us as a heritage. No man is lacking it, even in the most remote places on earth and therefore, has no excuse for walking in the darkness, for committing crimes, be the tormentor, slanderer, or deceiver of his fellow man. There is Light that screams in his inner being, guiding him to do what is good and just, towards greatness and prosperity, towards power and righteousness. It is an inheritance for everyone because it has been given to every man, without exception.

The First Thing is Not Change

The parable of The Prodigal Son tells us that when the young man came to the point of wanting to eat the food that the pigs were eating, "he came to his senses." When we analyze the story, we can see that the first thing was not "the change" the first thing was, "consciousness". This is the key to change: a state of awareness of who we are and where we are going. There are people who insist on convincing others to live like they think, and make the same changes that they have made, by using methods such as abuse, manipulation, offense, and humiliation.

Another phenomenon that occurs is that there are people who use their talents and persuasiveness for their own benefit, to the point that they convince others to make important decisions.

I want to advise you to be careful of those situations. Most people who are trapped in life, are not there because they are bad or indecisive, but because someone took them in a different way, and deviated them from their purpose.

When you feel that a person is persuading you to make a change in your life, don't accede immediately. Go to a place where you can be alone, in solitude, where you usually meet your inner self, where no one bothers you, where you can forget about the daily activities for a moment, and when you are in the stillness, ask yourself, what should I do? God always talks when we are silent. People cannot have inner power if they have fear or listen to external voices that bombard them constantly.

When the world is at risk and everything yours is in danger it is necessary to open your inner ears and listen. When you do, you can leave the darkness and live in the light.

Jesus was asleep in the stern while the boat was being beaten by the waves or a terrible storm. When his disciples woke him up, it says he called them, "men of little faith", stood up and rebuked the storm with these words, "Silence! Be still!" and the wind immediately died down.

Later I will talk in more detail about those words, but for now want I want to emphasize is that Jesus had power over the storm because he could be confident in the middle of the storm. No one can be confident in the midst of something that he does not control and of which he is afraid.

When a person is not sure about the changes that he is about to make but goes ahead anyway, because other people have forced him to do so, not only he will not go very far, but he will not remain standing when the storm comes. Many times I have made the mistake of doing things motivated by other people's words. In my inner being I felt I needed to wait, that it was not the right moment, that I had to look for my own strategies, but in the end I let myself to be persuaded. The result? It didn't work! And the storm that preceded me, put me in a world of much turbulence, the doubt flooded me, taking away the power of hearing my own inner Light, and producing results that I didn't want.

When your world is in danger, and everything that belongs to you is in danger, it is necessary that you open your inner ears and listen, it is the only way you can leave the darkness and go to the Light.

Many people have said to me, "I feel lost. I don't know what to do. I feel stuck in turbulence, even though I put a lot of effort to get out, I cannot find the way."

Some have said to me, "I don't know how I got into this

mess. I think it's because there is someone else involved in my decisions: my sister, my brother, my parents, some teacher, or a friend. Nothing of what I have done has been my own initiative. On the contrary, I have made decision forced by others, only to see myself later in a world of much confusion. But what is worse, is that those who persuaded me, act like nothing happened; I even have the impression that they have planned to get me into the mess, then act as if they are innocent."

The truth in this event is not that they are taking the role of the innocent, they are just thinking about their own problems and challenges. People cannot help us to make our decisions because they are not inside of us, and they don't know our purpose. People will talk to you based on their own experiences and their knowledge.

Everybody knows that in this world of conscious people there no two roads equal, there aren't two identical human beings, or two similar destinies. We can connect with other people to carry a common purpose, but we cannot forget individuality and variety. In a river, the same water doesn't come by twice. So is the man and his purpose, he will never repeat history, nothing will be the same after time has passed.

Change is something constant, whether you like it or not, because the world keeps moving and doesn't stop. In other words, when you feel an urge to do something good, be a part of some vision, join a certain group, or become a member of a certain church, etc., take time to think and ask yourself, why? What is moving me to do this? What will I accomplish, or be able to give, that is related to my purpose? The answers should always be related with your purpose. The Creator of everything will never move you to do anything or to go anywhere that is not related to accomplishing your purpose in life.

When Jesus and His disciples were in the boat, in the midst of that great storm, the disciples were fearful because experience told them that their boat would not stand up to the situation. Its entirely possible that some of their friend's names that had died in a storm came to their minds. But Jesus was asleep. From the moment He took the boat to cross the sea, he was aware that they would face a storm on the way.

This state of awareness, and your ability ponder about certain decisions, is what will give you the wisdom and the power in everything that you do. The conscience of man can only speak to the man who has it; therefore, cultivate the habit of listening to it, and you will see that the next time you find yourself in a project, in a situation, in a boat hit by the headwinds of life, you will be more aware of the power that you have. Change has power when we first enter a state of self-consciousness. When you are in the state of mind of knowing that you are "going to the other side," the Light that you have will not turn off, it will rule over all storms that you encounter on your way. This is the difference between a confused man and one who has clarity of mind. He who is confused doesn't cross to the other side; he who knows that he is there for a purpose, and his ways are illuminated by a Superior Being who will not let him fail, will have power over everything, and His Light will shine on everything he does.

Usually, during my conferences, I can leave the facility while the other speakers give their talks. But this one time I was invited to speak in the city of Virginia, and they asked me to remain in the room to listen to the other speakers.

After me, a man named Lauro gave his speech; he was from Mexico, and had been invited by the same company where he worked. His introduction of how he had started in the business didn't empress me much, but that didn't make it less real and exciting.

His was the typical case of those who find themselves in bankruptcy and don't know what to do, until finally, they find themselves at a dead end, and a door opens, a light shines, and they find hope. It is at that moment when God turns their lives around.

The story of Lauro struck me when I heard him saying that. First, he had a stable life when he entered into the business.

Second, when he was more excited about the business, everything started to collapse, and "the big, successful ones" who motivated him to get in when they were in the peak, they also collapsed.

Change has power when we first enter a state of self-consciousness.

Third, although he had entered the business because he had been influenced to do so, he remained in the business. But in reality that wasn't something he wanted to do.

And fourth, in spite of the many setbacks, he stayed in the business and after ten years he read a book that awoke something deep within him. An urgent sense of need obligated him to change. In a few months he had to attend some conferences in the United States and sitting on the plane he asked God to make him feel the same as when he came to the company, that He let him once again dream and become enthused, because he had lost his enthusiasm. He would attend the conventions and not feel any emotion.

There are people who deny the value of the good because they have only experienced the bad. There are people who don't believe that something good can happen to them because their past experiences weren't the best. If you are living an experience where you feel uncomfortable with what you have or where you are, it is because something within you demands a change.

When we constantly complain about a situation and we are not in agreement with what is happening to us it is because our conscience is screaming for change. The conscience needs to be activated in order to produce change.

When Lauro arrived at the convention, to his surprise, the main speaker was the same person who had written the book that had begun to awaken within him the desire to grow. God will always make a way for those who want to have a better life; but many times, people cannot have a better life because they don't desire to have it.

When he got back home, his wife asked him, "So, how did it go?" He just said, "¡I will be big!" and from that day forward he began to work towards that. In five years he achieved the goal that he had set in order to change his financial situation. When I saw him again, he had a good life; he was enjoying traveling all over the world and talking about his victories.

Why did that happen to this man? Because his conscience was awakened and he saw who he was, what he could accomplish. That was when he set about to conquer his dream.

Anything is possible when your conscience awakens to the knowledge of a change. The expansion of all the things is in the Light of the conscience that makes a man make changes and rule the kingdom of darkness.

The Power of Light

Chapter 3

The Light That
Attracts Success

Every successful person is made by traveling a long road. This is possible if they have worked hard for success. It is necessary to see something good in a world filled with darkness and negativity. You will need a Light to guide you to that end. This is what we call, "vision". Vision is the ability to see a better future. We will discuss this in upcoming chapters, but for now let me say that people with vision achieve success, and the only reason they do is because they can envision the outcome. Everything that the mind is capable of seeing and believing, it is capable of creating.

In the Dominican Republic there is a serious problem

in regards to the supply of I can remember the times I used to get up for a drink or to go to the bathroom. I would stretch my arm to pull the string attached to the light socket in order to turn on the light.

But many times that I pulled the string I had to face the fact that there was no electricity so the light would not come on. I would try to get out of bed in the dark, but I would end up banging my head, because without realizing it, I was getting out of the wrong side of the bed!

After dealing with that experience, I would change direction and get down from my bed very carefully. But it was more than once that I banged into chairs, tables and anything else that was in my way.

Other times I would kick the bed-pot and spill urine everywhere. Today, I can laugh about it, but those times were hardly laughing times.

Many people hope to achieve success in their marriage, business or organization. They hope to be happy and become outstanding human beings but they lack the capacity to see the way. They don't understand that without a vision there is no light to illuminate the way and they live in absolute darkness.

Every person has a light of self-improvement within but it needs to be activated. It is within each person, but it has to be lit. Paul said, "Do not extinguish the Spirit." The spirit of man has the power to fan the flame or extinguish the flame.

Jacob, the father of the twelve pillars of the tribes of Israel, had twelve children but only two of them were from Rachel, the woman he truly loved. Rachel died while giving birth to the second of the two and Jacob took on an obsession for his two sons, Joseph and Benjamin. Joseph was the oldest of the two. He was a restless boy and a dreamer.

> *Every person has a light of self-improvement within but it needs to be activated. It is within each person, but it has to be lit.*

One day he told his father and brothers, "I had a dream last night where there were twelve bundles of wheat all bowing down to me, and another dream where the moon and the stars also bowed to me." His father interpreted the dream to mean that Joseph was going to govern over them and he became upset with his son and reprimanded him in a scornful manner, "Young boy, you sure have a great imagination; why don't you find something better to do with it!" Jacob was a visionary, but even so he could not recognize the Light in the dreams of his son Joseph.

The people around you will never tell you, "You can do it!" And it is not because they don't desire success for you, but because they don't understand what goes on inside you and they was to steer you away from anything they think will cause you harm. To them, you are nothing more than the little brother, the neighbor from the corner or the friend they played with growing up. They know you and see your for your possibilities, and don't believe you are capable of something greater than what they already know you can do or than what they have been able to achieve.

You need to believe so strongly in your dreams that the light within you can be see on the outside.

Like the woman who gets pregnant the first night that she has sex. She knows if she is pregnant or not. Even though others may try to convince her that she isn't she knows that she is and she begins to do everything necessary to make sure that her child is protected and is born healthy.

If they say to her the following day, "You are not pregnant," she will still insist, "Oh yes I am!" Your job is to repeat to yourself over and over again, "Yes, it is possible." "Yes, I am going to do it." "Yes, I am going to have a son." "Yes, I am going to be successful." "Yes, I am healthy."

The woman who knows she is pregnant isn't worried about what people say of her neither is she concerned that they think she is not pregnant. She knows she is and that is all that matters. Why? Because she knows that all of those who don't believe her will soon see the evidence. When we dream within us and believe in those dreams, it matters little what others say and we will keep working to make those dreams come true.

The Light Bothers Those Who Are Blind

This is a principle that is applied to the world of business, economics, and developmental. Joseph, the son of Jacob, kept telling about his dreams, and what he would do when these dreams came true. This only served to increase the anger that his brothers held against him and they conspired to kill him, throwing him alive into an abandoned well. It was not that his brothers hated him; they hated the ideas of growth that he expressed. They could not admit that someone their minor could aspire greater things than they could.

People who don't have "the Light of Knowledge" and walk in the darkness of conformity, hate those who have the power to lighten the world in some sphere; they also hate those who have extraordinary ideas. Joseph knew of this principles that says, "They can kill you, but they can never kill your dreams!" Men and women who want to kill dreams are nothing more than empty wells. Empty wells are no good for anything.

The following day when the brothers uncovered the well and saw that Joseph had not died, they decided to sell him to some traveling merchants who happened to come by. These in turn sold Joseph to a captain of the Egyptian army, named Potiphar.

When this teenager arrived at the house of the captain of the palace guard, he was treated as a common slave. However, soon his light began to shine amongst those around him, and his master took notice, acknowledging that since bringing this young slave to his house, he had increasingly prospered because of him.

Seeing his abilities, his responsibility, his loyalty and his hard work, Potiphar began to reward him and put him in charge of his household, and all that he owned. But when everything was going smoothly, the wife of the master set a trap for Joseph, which put him out of favor with Potiphar, his trusting master. As a result, Joseph ended up in the king's prison. But even there in prison Joseph was responsible with his obligations and the prison guard put him in charge of all of the other prisoners.

Then the unexpected happened. Two important prisoners came to the prison: one was the king's bread-maker, and the other was his cup bearer. The two were prisoned on suspicion of conspiracy. These two men both dreamed one night and Joseph, who had the Light to interpret dreams was able to give the interpretation to each and as he predicted, they were fulfilled. The cup bearer was restored to his former position and the baker was killed. Even though the cup bearer promised Joseph he would put in a good word for him to the Pharoah, he completely forgot about him.

After two years the Pharoah dreamed a dream that none of his wise men could interpret. That was when the cup bearer remembered his promise to Joseph and spoke to the Pharoah about his innocence. He told the Pharoah of Joseph's ability to interpret dreams and as a result, Joseph was called, he gave the Pharoah the interpretation his needed, and he was elevated to the position of Prime Minister over all of the land of Egypt. There are sometimes circumstances that would cause you to believe that your dreams will never become reality, but these will surely come to pass if you don't stop believing.

Your dreams will always be fulfilled if you continue to believe in them and in the Eternal One. He put those dreams in your heart and he loves you too much to not fulfill them. The darkness of the envious and those who don't believe in you will try to eliminate the Light in you, perhaps even mocking you, maybe other times telling you that you are useless and incapable, even others pointing out your limitations and mistakes.

But if you are able to believe that within you there is a Superior Light, you will continue to fight for what you believe in. When you find yourself as a slave doing something you don't like, while you are on track to fulfill your dream to reach the goal of doing what you really would like to do in life...when you find yourself in a 'prison' of those who would take advantage of your talents and detour you from your purpose... it will be in those situations and amongst those type of people that want your downfall that you will do the best, without resorting to complaining or cursing your lot in life, while waiting for the birth of that dream deep within you.

Thirteen years went by until the dreams of Joseph became reality, until he finally saw his dreams came true. He didn't allow those who hate his Light to turn him off.

During my career of leadership, I have seen many people with bitterness and resentment because of the injustice of those who, taking advantage of their position, they took them out of work and sent them to a place with less privileges. Friend, don't let his happen. If you want to grow, you must know that growth is for those who shine; and anyone who shines will find an enemy who wants to turn off his Light.

There are sometimes circumstances that would cause you to believe that your dreams will never become reality, but these will surely come to pass if you don't stop believing.

While working to develop congregations in New York, I discovered that the mindset of the organization to which I belonged was not the same in the United States as it was in my country. There, they rewarded in a big way those who worked and met their goals.

When I arrived, my fellow colleagues had all kinds of excuses and pretexts. One of them was that here in the

United States people are indifferent and don't respond to the invitations of churches. I started to break all those patterns when I gave my first conference and the leaders decided to extend the event for another 21 days due to the large quantity of people that were in attendance.

That year not only was I the one to win more people for the organization, but I built up a new organization that broke the records for the past 100 years.

But all of this did not bring me happiness, but rather much pain and problems. Several colleagues rose up that bad-mouthed me everywhere, and it seemed like it didn't matter what I did or said, they would always find reason to make me look bad and try to destroy me.

In contrast to the rest, I got into radio and television, and was able to put my programs on radio stations and channels of national fame. But all of the proofs of my talent and the favor of God did not convince them, and they always found new ways to turn off my light and others besides them could easily see and appreciate.

One thing I did learn from that was that God always backed me up and there was a supernatural grace at work to win people. People loved me and supported me in an extraordinary manner. But this bothered many who thought that I was responsible for their lack of leadership and they kept looking for ways to through me in 'prison' or the 'dry well' of the ten envious brothers.

To put someone in prison you just need power, but to put someone in a palace, you need leadership. Leaders who are proud of the number of disciples that fell in disgrace, whether it was justifiable or not, have lost the true Light of leadership. True effective leadership is characterized by the number of disciples that grow, and not by those that end up as failures.

I remember being in a place where the people showed a special appreciation towards me. My director encouraged me to me to go to this place where for 19 years they had only achieved a growth of 19 people. He explained that there was nothing that could be done for that place. He said, "Just go there and visit some of the leaders so that they stop bothering and calling the office, but do not worry what others think because there, nobody has been able do anything and from those people no one can get good results."

With that in mind I went to the place, but when I arrived, as I always did, I got excited about the work in building up the leader in charge and the organization. I began to inspire him and the results were immediate. The congregation began to grow and multiplied greatly. The people saw something special in me and this inspired them by helping them to believe they could do better, which resulted in gradual but lasting changes.

But again some were not happy with what was happening. People were happy, the congregation was growing, but this did not inspire the enemies I had in the organization and neither did it change their attitude towards me. Instead, it made them angrier!

When you have the light of success within you as everything you do gives positive results, the average and mediocre people are bothered; not because you are against them or stealing something from them, but because it is too humiliating for them. My intention was not to make anyone look bad and had no desire to humiliate or take away something, but for some reason they saw it that way. Many of them spoke of me with so much anger that if they had had a chance to kill me, I'm sure they would have.

The previous leader, the one who had achieved a growth of 1%, would call constantly to the other leaders warning them to be careful of me because I was working with occultism and hypnotism from a foreign culture. Today, that comment wouldn't bother me, but at the time, it did. Soon, the main organization moved me from there, and it was always that way. They would take me from one place to another, until I made the decision to go to a different place, and start a process of transformation and healing (not pleasant at all), but in the end it became a great blessing to my life. When you walk in the Light there is no darkness that can overshadow you.

It doesn't matter what kind of darkness is after your success or the inspiration that is within you—call it envy, hatred, anger, selfishness—what I can assure you is that if you don't get resentful with God, or with the world, if you keep believing, if you make the necessary changes in your life, you will triumph because you were created to triumph and only you can keep that from happening.

Those who fear the envious and the egotists who don't love triumph and who get offended when someone else achieves, will never reach their purpose and they will remain on the earth saying, "I couldn't do it because X, Y and Z persons who didn't help me achieve my purpose in life. That "I couldn't" is more painful and humiliating than all of the criticism of the world.

There Will Always Be Two Groups

The world will always have two kinds of people: some negative and some positive. There are those that carry light within them and others that see nothing. The people who have light try to get out of ignorance and break the limits of the past. Education creates a solid foundation and you can always unlearn what has been learned. When I refer to education I am not talking about university education, although I don't minimize university level studies.

Rather, I am talking about the true education that comes from within a person who is open and desires more; a man or a woman that does not conform and that does not accept that all records have been broken and that all that is left for him or her is death. We can learn from anyone, all of us are as open books and we need to appreciate each and every one. But there are people who by their own choice have decided to walk in constant darkness.

It is that the darkness only loses its power on man when there is the presence of Light, and the Light is brighter the darker the darkness.

There is in our universe an expressed truth that no man who truly wants to grow can ignore, because there are two undeniable masses of energy that make a perfect harmony and that permit the existence of everything we observe. One is "black energy" and the other is "the energy of light". It is important to apply this same knowledge to things here on earth.

The truth is that even though many of us complain and at times consider insignificant the contribution of those living in their vices, those who don't aspire to anything better, those who are homeless and wander the streets begging...I want to assure you that their contribution is very significant because they give value and conscience to those who desire to live differently. That is why I dare to say that they have a number of things to teach us. It is that the darkness only loses its power on man when there is the presence of Light, and the Light is brighter the darker the darkness.

Prisons should not be places of regret, such as sickness, pain, poverty and homelessness. Why? Because that is the place or state where we can shine more. You say, "But Wilson, you do not think you're talking about exploiting the needy." No way, I'm talking about shinning; growing to inspire others with our light. There is no virtue in staying hidden, in not advancing, but we cannot avoid that for different reasons many do.

This should not be a reason to be sad, but to reflect. For two reasons: first, because we can inspire them; and second, because we can learn from that state of life and say this is not the life I want to live. While it is true that the world becomes increasingly uncertain, so it is when people do not let their lamp of light go out.

Mother Teresa of Calcutta said: "Sometimes what we do is like a drop of water falling in the middle of the ocean, but the ocean would be smaller without it." I have seen how many people let the darkness put their light out. People say to me, "I do not give what's mine to anyone, much less to those who beg in the streets, because it is just to maintain their vices." Others tell me, "I don't believe anyone in this world, there are too many bad people and liars." And so I could spend much time enumerating different facts and reasons of why many people do not help but these facts should not put out your lamp of giving.

I was in Portland, Oregon, giving seminars on communication and relationships. The young man who was responsible for taking me to the hotel and wherever I needed to go, pointed at a man on one of the corners of the streets of Portland.

While observing the homeless man he said to me, "Look

at this man begging…he could be working. Anything he did would get him more than begging, but of course, those type are without vision and full of vices." I looked at him and asked, "How many hours a day does this man stay here?" He said, "From 12 to 14 hours a day, to take home maybe $15 to $20." "There's the problem," I said to him. "The man is working more than he is paid for." "Working?" he answered me. "He is not working, he is begging." "Look at it from a different angle, from a positive perspective," I replied. "This man could rob, assault or kill someone to take something from them, but he prefers to beg. He spends 14 up to 14 hours a day begging, so he doesn't hurt anyone; that is something to admire."

There is something here that needs to be learned and that those who call ourselves "normal' never take into account. The first is that this man prefers to suffer all kinds of rejection, cold, sun, rain, hunger, thirst, etc., to get some money, rather than harm someone. There has to be some good in that dark and confused soul to do something like that.

The second is the attitude displayed by the vast majority of people that prefer to pass this man by, ignoring him, not giving him even a single penny. These same people who pass him by ignoring him, if they were assaulted by the same person and he put a gun to their chest or a knife to their throats would beg him for their lives. And they would not only say they were willing to give him all the money on them, but that they would not tell anyone if he would only spare their lives. But because this guy stands on the corner begging without demanding, they don't give him anything. I believe that if all of us were to give, say $2 a month to help the needy people in a country such as ours who live in darkness in regards to success and don't live a normal or healthy lifestyle, we would not have as much violence in our society.

This example is only related this problem, but the principle itself doesn't just apply to those who beg but also for those who have no hope. Why? Because "the Light ruled over the darkness and the darkness had no more power over the Light."

I want to make it clear to you that there will always be two groups of people: one that is in constant growth and in control of things, and the other, of misery, poverty, anarchy and out of control.

If those of us who have received the Light in order to understand that there is a better world, we will use it to help to make it happen, using our energy of love and greatness to touch those in need causing them to wake up and stop focusing only on the negative things of life.

In the story of Joseph, Jacob's son, when he was taken out of jail, and put in second command in the kingdom, he sent for his father and his brothers from the land of Canaan to have them participate with him in his joy and greatness. Joseph's brothers shined in the history of Israel and the ancient world, not for their vision and goodwill, but for that of a brother who didn't become resentful.

When his brothers went to his house with fear and told him the act of cruelty they had committed, and that they had sold him, Joseph said, "I don't hold it against you, I don't have resentment towards you, nor will I seek revenge. The evil that you planned against me became the path to achieve my vision, and it is possible that this was the method that God used to save many."

A successful man is not only a person who has done well in life, but he who admits that he doesn't have anything to worry or resent in life, because everything that happens to him in this world is on his side, and everything that happens to him is for a good reason. We will never be able to exterminate in a radical way all of the evil in the world, but we can react with positive thoughts towards those who touch our lives and they ours.

Success is for those who dream and those who have visions. But true success is for those whose dreams are not blurred by egotism, greed, arrogance and hatred, but rather they no how to value others and they are committed to love and living by principles, and good and pure values.

> *True success is for those whose dreams are not blurred by egotism, greed, arrogance and hatred.*

A successful man is a happy man, because he is loyal to his friends, to his principles, to his company, and to humanity. He knows he is here in the world for a greater purpose. He knows that if he came into this world in contrast to many who died before birth, it is because the Light of life is on his side. That is why he chooses to live grateful, and live his life to the fullest.

Chapter 4

The Power of Darkness

While we have said that darkness has less power than Light, but nonetheless it does have power and we cannot deny that fact. To ignore reality in regards to certain matters is not living positively, but ignorantly.

Once example of this is that I will not have power over gravity by ignoring it, but rather by studying it and observing what other laws have more power than it does. The knowledge of this fact will benefit me greatly. This is how we are able to travel from one country to another in a metal box that today we call an 'airplane'. This science is known as the Law of Aerodynamics.

When I refer to the power of darkness I am speaking about all of the evil that affects our world today and is part of the dominant ignorance that prevails. In the natural realm we could take into consideration dark matter or dark energy both of which have power to keep things in equilibrium. This is an important topic in regards to the physical realm and modern cosmology, however, what we call dark matter or dark energy is likewise a description of our ignorance. In other words, it is a way that the scientific community describes what they can't explain yet. There are only theories and no one knows what these matters are made of and that is why they use terms like that to describe something so mysterious in the universe.

This principle applies in all of the earth: the struggle against evil, the abuse of drugs, alcohol, poverty, hunger and other bad things that affect our planet. It is a way of making us live a productive life with meaning, because the presence of these evils causes us to prepare ourselves to confront them each and every day in our lives. It sounds like I am saying that evil is necessary in order for good to reign.

And in a certain way that is true, because without darkness, light has no meaning, or at least we minimize its importance. The thicker the darkness, the more powerful that light is. The sicker we are, the more we appreciate being healthy. The more needy people there are, the more we appreciate what we have. Adam and Eve did not appreciate clothing because they did not realize they were naked, because "they were naked and they were not ashamed." But when their eyes were opened to this knowledge, then "they realized they were naked and they sewed fig leaves to cover themselves."

It is important that we understand that we will not achieve anything by complaining of the evils that ravage our world and the power of those who do wrong. On the contrary, we should let our light shine brighter and in that way be more appreciated, for we are not here on the earth to complain about our lot in life, but to appreciate who we are, what we do and what we represent. Darkness does not take away the Light, on the contrary, it gives Light more power.

When I was little, most of the time I used to get up at noon, right when my mother was finished making lunch. It was the perfect moment for my brothers and I to take advantage of the opportunity and play our game of "selling the food." We would sell it to one another for leaves that we considered money. To us, the food didn't have any meaningful value; we simply made a game of it with the price of leaves.

When I began to take responsibility in life and married Sandra, she gave me three sons and they don't give much importance to food either. Many times I prepare sandwiches for them which they push to one side and don't eat but which I paid good money for. That is why I try to encourage them not to turn up their noses at food and to have more appreciation for it.

Appreciation for anything depends on the Light and the knowledge acquired about it. Mother Teresa of Calcuta said, "The person who takes a bath is not he who is more dirty, but he who is more aware of cleanliness." The darkness is powerful over those who cannot see the Light because they walk in darkness.

The Power of Darkness

Darkness Causes Panic

Fear doesn't come from knowledge but from ignorance. When I was a child I was so afraid of the dead that many times I couldn't sleep at night.

One day, my grandmother sent me to a warehouse that was about 6 kilometers away from our house, and it got dark before I was able to make it back home. It was so dark that I could barely distinguish the path home, and I was so afraid that I could hardly breathe. While I was walking through a coffee field, the fireflies lit up the way, but my parents had scared me by saying that those light-bearing insects came from Purgatory and they were the souls of those that could not find rest.

So with each step through the coffee field the idea that these insects came from the other world kept gnawing at me and my fear increased like a thermometer in the heat. But when something fell from the trees I began to run scared, and the more I ran the more scared I got. I was running so fast because it seemed that someone from the grave was about to catch me. There were times I could feel their breathing on me and other times like their hands were about to choke me. I was so scared I began to scream. I cried out, "HELP! HELP ME!! A dead man is going to eat me!!!" I kept screaming that and I ran as fast as I could.

As I remember that now, I realize I was running from my own fears, my false beliefs and my ignorance about the condition of the dead. This was what made me think that they could come back and scare the living, but the truth is that the dead have no power that the living don't give them. That is why it is very important that you understand that only the living kill the dead.

But in life, there are many people who run from things that don't exist. They live a life of fear with no meaning, and they cause themselves fear from false beliefs. Running doesn't make a person safer. Running doesn't take you to the next level. It only helps you to avoid reality. We can survive by avoiding reality, but not truly live.

True life requires courage, tenacity and being aware of the present. It requires you to stop and face excuses, false beliefs, fears, and everything that is dark inside of us.

We cannot live a good life when we are controlled by feelings of failure. Many people run through life without seeing any results. They know that they need something better, but there is a superior power that detains them. That power is called fear and it has the same power as faith.

Later I will discuss in more detail about this matter, because I believe it is very important, but for now, what I want you to know is that fear is a power of darkness.

The Bible says that when Jesus entered the upper room where the disciples had hidden for fear, they did not recognize him because they were full of fear—they feared for their lives. But Jesus appeared to them and said:

"Peace be with you" and gave them a declaration that transformed their lives for good: "Receive the Holy Spirit. What you bind on earth will be bound in heaven, and you will have authority to forgive." These words gave the disciples a knowledge they did not have before, and caused them to put away their fears, leave their hideout, and go out and conquer the world.

> *Running doesn't take you to the next level. It only helps you to avoid reality.*

By the large number of Christians that are in the world, and the lands that were conquered by Christianity, we know that these men were motivated by a strong conviction. But my point is that were there is darkness, there is ignorance and where there is ignorance, there is fear.

The lack of understanding of who you are and what your purpose is what causes you to live a life filled with confusion and darkness.

Darkness Makes You Be Just One More

In the neighborhood where I grew up as a kid they decided to protest the fact that it was almost one year that we had been without electricity and the electric company did nothing to fix the problem.

I belonged to a religious group that did not allow people to join in the protest against the government. But people's desperation was so great that all of the leaders in the church decided that we should join the protest. As a matter of fact, all of the other denominations and organizations also joined the cause.

Things became so serious that it was like unforgivable heresy not to be a part of the strike. At night we would go out to cut down trees and block the streets and in this way make a visible divide of the territory. Many times we would use the herds of cows from the neighboring farms to stampede and chase away the police.

I remember the time I arrived late because of staying up late the night before, cutting down trees to block traffic through the area. But the police chased us and I, when it had to do with running, did so with all my expertise and energy. But that night was particularly dark. I was running like greased lightning, but not being able to see well broke off some branches with my delicate chest—at that time in my life I weighed somewhere around 109 to 116 pounds, stood over 6 feet tall, and looked like a toothpick. Some confused me with a giraffe. My long arms, and my muscular legs of 14 centimeters around, gave me an aspect of a grasshopper and of course, I lived up to that image.

So, to continue the story, that morning I left the house late in the day and I headed for the command center that was at the beginning of the bridge that divided our neighborhood from the rest of the city.

While I was walking, a saw a large crowd that was running towards me and yelling voices of desperation. Bewildered, I instantly joined them, not asking any questions, and with the same look of fear that I saw in everyone else, I also began shouting from the top of my lungs to anyone I saw, "Ruuuuuuuuuuuuuuunnn!!!! Ruuuuuuuuuuuuuuuuuuuun!!!!!!!!" The more we ran, the more people joined the running mob.

We all had the same look of fear and no one stopped to ask if they should do it or not. They just ran and encouraged others that they met on the road to do the same.

When I was almost out of breath for running so fast for so long, I saw a friend at my side as if trying to beat me running to see who could get there first. So I asked him, "Hey, John, what happened?" He answered breathlessly,

"Someone hit the captain with a stone and he is coming after us. The police said that anyone they catch they will beat them to death."

My friend had barely finished telling me that, then my bony legs felt someone had put rocket engines from Apollo 11 on them. I didn't see my friend after that because I ran like the bionic man and soon I was at home hiding under my bed, where I stayed for quite some time.

The truth is a Light; a lie is a darkness.

It was probably two hours later when I gradually started to come out, like a mouse that sticks his head out looking one way and the other before crossing the street. To my surprise others were sticking their heads out and others were already walking freely up and down the street laughing about the exciting adventure.

So now, what had looked like bull-run with everyone running for their lives turned into something funny! So I asked, "Why is everything so funny?" So they explained things to me. "Everything was a joke by someone who wanted to go home or who was bored to death. They started to run and scream that they had hit the captain with a stone so everyone started to run with them."

Today, as I look back, I find this story funny. But the memory of this event doesn't remain in my memory for the funniness but for how scared I was and because it taught me a valuable life lesson. I learned to not follow others just for the sake of following them. I learned not to believe what other people tell me, even when it seems that what they are saying is true. Why?

Because in life, people run like those people of my neighborhood, they run without knowing why they are running. The young man who started the "great run" knew that it was a lie, but the lie was so powerful, even he did have the power to stop it. As more and more people joined the panicked mob, I think that even he began to believe the story, running with the rest of the people, and warning others about the danger. It was a lie that had become a truth.

In life we live limited lives because others limit us. They tell us stories based on lies, but we decide to believe them. The truth is a Light; a lie is a darkness. "You shall know the Truth and the Truth will set you free." People live running with the crowd, but they don't realize what they are doing, because their conduct has been culturally taught to them. Many like to buy a house similar to the others, a car that is popular, and we run with the same ideas, phrases and talk like the crowd.

To get out of the "status quo" requires one to stop and find out the truth, but we are afraid that the truth may kills us, or that it may be unpleasant and affect us, so we prefer to remain in darkness, because is more easy to be friends with everybody than to be friends with the Light.

To be one of the bunch, think like everybody else, believe that we have the absolute truth, refuse any kind of change and resist to any kind of knowledge, is being part of the crowd and live a dangerous darkness.

John, one of the close friends of Jesus, described the power that the darkness has on most people when he said: "The true Light that gives light to every man was coming into the world. He was in the world, and though the world was made through him, the world did not recognize him." But John the baptizer, who dressed in camel skins and lived in the desert, recognized him for who He was.

I bring out the fact that amongst so many people, only one man was able to recognize that Light because it provides proof that when you live by what others think, even those who say they are intelligent will not be a light in the midst of a dark multitude of people. When you limit yourself to false or old beliefs, swallowing them whole as gospel truth, you will find yourself enveloped in mediocrity and stagnation.

The men who followed Jesus are famous today because they recognized a greater knowledge than that of their era, culture, knowledge, and religion, and they followed it. Everyone else remained in darkness and disappeared in time and history. A greater revelation will precede the one you already know. Don't reject it but rather recognize it and walk in it.

Darkness Obscures Our Way

When I was little I suffered unexplained and frequent fevers. Time and time again they would come back during different times in my life. Because we lived in the countryside, and the lack of knowledge of my parents regarding the dangers of high fevers in the brain of a child, nothing was done to discover the reason for these painful episodes.

Fevers became more and more frequent, causing me negative effects, from which I only remember some. I remember there were times when I did not know where I was, even though I was in my bed. Sometimes I got out of bed to swim in the river (after listening to a voice that told me to do it).

Sometimes I would be walking in a path, apparently conscious, when I would go in a different way, or even walk in a place that was not even a path but rather bushes and cow fences). Suddenly, I would realize that I was in the middle of the cows, and that I needed to get back to the path.

As long as I had these limiting beliefs, I would think that witches had a plan to suck out my blood or take possession of me. But later, when I was in fifth grade and I had learned to read and write, I learned about the power of the will after reading about men who had made important scientific advances on behalf of the rest of humanity.

One of those stories that impacted me was the life of Robert Hooke who discovered the cell. He was a sickly man, but his condition didn't hinder him. On the contrary, he exercised strict self-discipline to control his nervous tics. He also suffered from severe headaches, however, he was able to overcome his pain and went on to become a famous scientist.

I discovered that Beethoven composed one of his best masterpieces after losing his hearing. But it was not happenstance, but rather after he stopped worrying about it, because all of his life his worst fear was of going deaf.

I had good teachers, who took it upon themselves to teach me principles besides the classroom subjects. It was as if they felt a certain concern for me regarding certain divine principles that I needed to learn at an early age.

I honor my father, but I comprehend that his limited knowledge due to his upbringing. My mother always was concerned about my education and instilled in me the desire to learn. The both did what they could.

With this personal understanding I came to the conclusion that my mind was deceiving me. For some reason my mind worked with my fear, causing me to run from reality and taking me to a world of fantasy. It was then that I decided to take control of my mind and return from my unreal state of mind, which had put my life in danger, to reality.

My parents didn't understand the seriousness of this mental disorder, because they thought it only had something to do with the frequent fevers I had. Most of this they had no idea was happening, because I kept it quiet. The truth is that the fevers were a consequence of my fears. I attracted all of my evils. If I heard that someone was sick, I would get sick. If I heard a horror story, I would cover myself from head to toe and not sleep a wink. My mind produced images and emotions that made me live in a dark world that know one else knew of.

It was then that I decided to live in the light, begin to work with my mind and not accept its prognosis. My father had to hold me while I calmed down. With time I learned to conquer my mental condition. I did I by touching the bed when I would lie down, passing my hand over my surrounding to assure myself that I was in a physical place. When I would hallucinate, I would tell my mind that I was not falling anywhere, but that I was on the bed and that was my safety.

At first, it seemed this was not going to work, but the more I did it, the more I was able to take control of my world, the more I was able to leave the darkness and enter the light of living normal. Then the moment came that I was able to maintain complete control. When I would perceive that I was in something that was not mine and fear would take ahold of me, I would take conscious control of my thoughts and the space that I was in.

This experience was not only when I was awake, but I was also able to achieve control even of my dreams. I suffered from horrible nightmares, like falling out of trees, chased by the dead and ghosts that would chase me and I was helpless to defend myself. So I began to take control of the dreams that would scare me or were not for my good. I would talk to myself by taking control of my mind and saying to myself, "Wilson, you are dreaming and you need to wake up." That is how I would wake up from those dreadful dreams that were not good for me.

To this day I continue to do this. Every time I dream something that does not go with my life, my principles, my purposes, or if I have a nightmare, I speak to my mind, "It is just a dream, and it is time to wake up."

The knowledge of my problems and understanding that I had to power to fight against them, and the awareness that I had absolute control over my inner world, helped me conquer my inner demons and return to the real world. I could have, as many, remained in my dark world, in my inner world which would have kept me living reality for the rest of my life. But the light that was in me took charge and I conquered by the knowledge of my will.

When we remain profoundly calm, in solitude and silence, we develop the greatest of all powers, because it is in this power where the illusion is generated and this gives way to the real conscience.

If you don't take time to relax and fine tune your mind by means of connecting with your Creator, you could be creating a false illusion that will take you to a horrible reality.

The Darkness Makes You Live Below Who You Are

I met a young girl who was very good student. She had a big desire to succeed and live a better life. She registered at the university and started to study hard, but one day, someone entered her room and raped her. After this horrible event, she thought that everybody was following her and wanted to rape her everywhere she went, and the demon was looking for her to take her to hell. To this day she has lived a miserable life. She has been in and out of psychiatric hospitals.

Something dark happened to this young girl, and darkness overwhelmed her Light. She could no longer see reality. The only way she could find relief was using strong drugs the doctors would prescribe for her.

This young girl had a dark moment and it created a dark history. That history had more power over her than any desire of improvement. She quit her studies and confined herself to living a life of hate and bitterness.

Some will say, "Wilson, are you saying we are responsible for what happens to us?" No, we are not responsible for everything that happens to us externally, but internally, yes we are. The interior is more powerful than the exterior. To every man and woman on the earth things happen, but not everyone has the same story.

Repeating a negative story again and again creates a negative world.

The events that happen to men don't destroy them, but rather the story that we tell over and over until it becomes reality and creates a world inside our world is what destroys us. Repeating a negative story again and again creates a negative world.

Words have power, because these words are spirit. Jesus, the Master said: "The words I have spoken to you are spirit and they are life." People create a world of demons, monsters, hatred, grudges, resentments, bitterness and they start living inside this world.

This monster that is tormenting you is your own creation. You did so with your beliefs and your words. You entered a dark world, you started to tell a story of that world and now you see it everywhere. I am not arguing whether or not there are legitimate mental illnesses but rather the majority of the things that we see and live we ourselves create with our own minds. And the worst part of it is that we go around trying to find someone else to put the blame on, believing our own made up lie. But power does not come from hate and lies, but rather from the Truth.

The darkness will always have power over you, unless you change your way of thinking. When you change your way of thinking, you will change your story. And if this is about power and faith, it will create a force greater than your own and will protect your world.

This was the power that God gave us. The power to be victorious over everything through the power of faith, and to create what we propose we want to do, through our words. "Without faith it is impossible to please God." The word "impossible" in this context means, "impotent".

Personally, I think that without faith we make God like our own image, we make him "impotent" because "… everything is possible for he who believes." Faith designs for us what we can achieve, but words reveal it. Faith is revealed in your words: "because as a man thinks, so is he…" and "…out of the overflow of his heart, his mouth speaks." If your thoughts are of faith, your words and your story will also be of faith. "If you have faith as small as a mustard seed, you can say to the mountain, 'move from here to there' and it will move."

We can see clearly that the manifestation of the power of the Creator in this world of men is about the Light of faith. Man decides how far he will go. He decides what he is going to see manifested in his world. He decides what kind of life he would like to live. In another chapter I will discuss this further.

But I want to make it clear to you that if you are living below what you should live you need to stop telling that old story and start creating a new one. Men of vision are not ones who go about telling a story, but rather those who go about creating one, and every man who is born in this world has the power to create one.

In conclusion, I will say that it's true that darkness has power, and many decide to be slaves of it, but don't forget that you are a being of Light, and it just takes a little bit of Light to remove darkness. Light is within you, and you have power over any situation or problem you may be facing. It doesn't matter if it is internal or external, you can overcome whatever you want, and become anything you want to become.

I am talking about what is internal, but remember that he who overcomes the internal obstacles has life to the fullest. Only what is in your inner being has control and power over you. Remember that I call "darkness" to all traumas and fears that control you and take your joy away, to everything that casts a shadows you, everything that makes your life shorter.

It's true that in the universe there exists a black mass and dark energy, but man and every known living being don't live there. Living beings are nurtured in Light, and their lives only are lasting where Light reigns.

Drops of Energy

When you analyze man's brain, it is similar to the universe. The active neurons look like a lighted city. When a brain ages, many neurons die and the image is that of a city that is shutting down, with many light bulbs burned out. The brain has Light because it keeps itself connected to energy.

Even more than that, our whole body is energy. The universe is energy. The substance of God is energy. And those who have had a genuine encounter with Him can corroborate this fact. "God is spirit, and his worshipers must worship him in spirit and truth." This is one of the reasons why I say that all of our faculties were created for us to have communication with the Light and be focused toward this.

Man's thoughts are no exception. We should not entertain evil or dark thoughts because these will dominate our emotions. As go our thoughts, so go our emotions. This is because thoughts are as drops of water that fill the ocean of the mind, so if they are bad thoughts they dirty the water, if they are clean thoughts, they keep it clean.

Thoughts also are as drops of energy that produce power in the emotions, and these in turn can produce energy or weakness in the body. A person can feel weak or energetic, depending on the thoughts that are going through the mind.

When you accumulate a lot of worries, your bodily energy diminishes and you start to feel brain-drain. This is why the fact remains that the majority of illnesses don't originate in the body but rather in the mind, by means of the thoughts. These produce mental images and trigger circumstances, because like attracts like.

Images produce emotions. Emotions are easier to detect than thoughts. Many authors said that we can put our mind in a blank state through profound meditation. I don't believe we can do so. I think that we can make our mind to concentrate on an image, and work with the thoughts by freezing a mental picture. I also think we can slow down our thoughts, but we cannot stop them completely. The mind can never be completely empty. When people think that they are not thinking, they are only ignoring reality. The mind is a system of gears that generate thoughts.

Man and His Thoughts

You are what you think. Your thoughts form your life and your future. People talk and do according to what they think. "As a man thinketh, so is he." People speak and do as they think, and every man and woman in this world needs to be conscious of that fact.

Socrates said that the purpose of philosophy was to make people think for themselves. For Socrates, the power of a teacher was to bring a man to understand his own power within. The disciple was to reach the place of trusting his own inner thoughts and by means of inner reflection, align his mind with his purpose and destiny.

Because of our upbringing and habits, we don't always think as we should. We have the bad habit of thinking according to our circumstances and situations around us. We fill our mind with those thoughts without realizing that we are being judged by the same. Why? Because our words and our actions come from our thoughts.

We say things we don't want to, because we allow ourselves to be driven by the thoughts that weigh us down. "From the abundance of the heart the mouth speaks." Many people worry more about the external appearance than the inner beauty. The truth is that the external is important but only if it is a consequence of the inner.

One day, Jesus sat to eat with his disciples and the Pharisees (the important religious people of that time). They criticized him because his disciples were breaking tradition by supposedly eating with dirty hands. So he said to them, "Don't you understand that everything that enters the mouth goes into the stomach and is cast out into a latrine? But what

> *The mind needs to be cultivated like a garden and the fruit of the mind is the thoughts.*

comes from the mouth originates in the heart... because from the heart proceed evil thoughts...this things contaminate men..." There are those who put a lot of important on what goes in their mouth and the aspect of their personality, but the important thing here is not the personality and such, but on how you think, what you have inside you and what you focus your thoughts on.

Thoughts are like food. Food nourishes our physical

body, while thoughts feed our spiritual body which is in the mind. Food has value when it nourishes our physical body. If you don't eat well, your physical body will suffer some illness or some upset. Exercise, nourishment and water play an important role in the physical realm, but only thoughts play an important role in the spiritual, the inner man. What we read, the images that we see and put in the mind as well as what we hear is what is transcendental in all of this.

If you analyze it, people more and more want things quick, shallow and lacking in imagination. Musical genres are based more on the rhythm than the words, and if there are words, they say little. This just goes to prove a point, that people nowadays don't like to spend time thinking. I am not against a particular genre of music because I think that in and of themselves, there is nothing wrong with any of them. But when this is the musical taste of the majority of people, good thought processes and good words are put aside to sing or say any morbid thought that comes to mind. That is when we need to be concerned.

The mind needs to be cultivated like a garden and the fruit of the mind is the thoughts. I have worked a lot with people who suffer from depression, and all these people have something in common: a dark past that they don't want to leave behind. They dwell in the sad things of the past, and on the flaws they have. Trying to tell them to surrender their past is like telling them: "Let's be enemies!"

Maybe you are a person that suffers from depression and maybe yours is chronic depression. The doctors have diagnosed and prescribed medications, and maybe even you have been hospitalized over and over again. You believe that you can't get out of this situation and you have resigned yourself to this way of living, thinking and telling yourself, "What else can happen to me! This is my destiny and fate in life. I'm just destined to suffer, cry and live from one bad experience to another." If that describes you… yes, I am writing this for you. I want you to know that that is a lie of the dark world! This feeling does not come from the world of Light and you should not believe it for one minute.

You will say, "But Wilson, that is a medical diagnostic!" Yes, but even though the medical community has worked and progressed according to revelation in the kingdom of Light, medicine only treats the body.

Thoughts are spiritual, and influence the mind. Paul

said, "You were taught, with regard to your former way of life, to put off your old self, which is being corrupted by its deceitful desires." There are thoughts and deceitful desires that keep us from seeing the greatness that we possess. They come from out past, from our culture and from our beliefs.

When we work on our thoughts and start to believe something good can happen to us, everything begins to change and we become different people. The patterns of conduct, emotions, illnesses and even chronic depression can disappear if you change your way of thinking. If you change the thoughts of fear to thoughts of peace…if you change thoughts of defeat to thoughts of victory, you will be a different person.

Thoughts and Emotions

While I was giving a conference in Atlanta, Georgia, the leader of the organization said to me that there was a woman who wanted talk with me. I met with her and her husband in a meeting room in the hotel and the first thing she said to me was, "I don't know where to begin…its that my story would take forever to tell you. So many negative things have happened to me, one after another…ever since I can remember, only bad things have happened to me."

At that moment I interrupted her and said, "Why don't you begin at the end and just forget telling me all of your life?"

"Well," she said, "the last thing that happened to me was that I had a heart attack and I lost feeling on my left side. They operated on this leg, they diagnosed me with cancer, all of the joints in my body ache, I have severe headaches…I have a husband but we never dated. I don't get ahead in anything, and I have financial problems. I have lost all interest in living, and one thing after another happens to me; I suffer from chronic depression."

She spoke about so many things that the list was endless. This, according to her, was the latest list of things to happen to her and when she finished telling me these things, without letting me say a word, she began from the beginning. She began to tell me back from when she could first remember anything.

As a little girl her parents abandoned her, and she had to live her childhood in a home where she was mistreated, sexually abused and made her feel like the most miserable little girl on the planet. She told me that when she began to develop, her godfather started to abuse her sexually.

Her husband, who was sitting close by, would say something once and awhile, and just looked at her with sadness in his face, nodding his head in agreement with what she said. He looked like he was more depressed than she was. People infect everyone next to them with their emotions and depressive conversations, which are a product of similar thinking.

At one point in telling her story she looked at her husband and said, "I went with this man at the age of 16. We never dated; I didn't even know him. I went because I didn't have any place to go and I needed to get out of that house."

I knew what she was telling me. What she wanted to say was, "I never even married the ideal man; I married a man I don't love, only because I had no other options."

This was a soul in total darkness, a person without any hope at all. All she could do was think about her past; remember everything that had happened to her to let it all out through her mouth. She didn't realize she was re-living her past emotions and mental state. It never occurred to her that every time she thought about that painful past she would bring bad things into her life. There was the essence of her problems, her depression, her cancer, her attacks and her fears.

When people live something negative or are going through difficult times, they think that telling their story all the time will help them find deliverance from the destructive emotions that weigh on them. But such is not true; they tell their stories because their emotions control them. Why? Because emotions were charged with painful thoughts of shame, failure and defeat.

The best way to realize that we are thinking in a negative manner is when our emotions are down, and when we feel sad or depressed. These will always be the result of our distorted way of thinking.

I began to talk to her about mental images and of the importance of changing those mental images, but in order to be able to do that one has to elevate the bad thoughts to become good thoughts. She had to change history, and to do that she had to imagine herself happy. This is what I told the woman, that she needed to visualize herself with everything that she desired. She needed to put images in her mind and see herself as her Creator saw her, full of love, of care, and with everything that she desired.

I explained to her that that was the meaning of living in faith, and living like that was living believing that life has good things for us. I proposed she start mental exercises of positive visualization and declare positive words of wellbeing over her life.

I also asked her to name the people that she needed to forgive. I wanted her to learn that she had work to do in order to distance herself from her horrible memories of her past that kept her in bondage. If she was not willing to forgive those who had harmed her, she would never find freedom from the bondage she was living under. If she really wanted to change her history it would require daily discipline.

You can pray, sing, beg and do all kinds of rituals, but if the thoughts are not renewed on a daily basis, nothing will be of any use to you. In the book of Romans we find this declaration, "Do not conform any longer to the pattern of this world, but be transform by the renewing of your mind, then you will be able to rest and approve what God's will is – His good, pleasing and perfect will." What it means is that when we want a change, we have to work on it.

Finally, the woman did everything that I asked her to do, accepting the declarations, my prayers and my exercises. In the end, I put my hand on her shoulder, I looked her in the eye and told her: "I declare God's peace over you." And she fainted.

She was out for more than half an hour. She could not move or stand up. I told her husband to stay by her side. Then I went to my hotel room to get my luggage because I had to catch a plane back to New York.

On my way out, through the hotel corridor, I found them. Her face shone and radiated happiness. She approached me and said: "God has a day for every person, and today was mine. Since Saturday morning when I saw you talking, I knew that there was something marvelous in you. You were shining with such grace that was very different from other motivators; your words were filled with power and a superior conviction. Now I feel different, I feel like someone took a load off me, that ripped something very dark from my soul, I feel like I am floating."

Dear reader, this is what I call being a Being of Light. If you know who you are and what you can give; if you focus your thoughts on that truth instead of focusing on the lies of past experiences, you are on your way to shine. The woman was sad and sick because that what she was in her mind.

When we change our way of thinking, everything changes, especially our emotions. That's where everything begins. If you change your thoughts you change your mental image. If you change your mental image, you also change your words and your acts. If you change your acts you will also change your habits and they will change your destiny.

The woman began to feel like her whole word had changed when she focused on the positive things I told her.

if you focus your thoughts on that truth instead of focusing on the lies of past experiences, you are on your way to shine.

Personally, I believe that everything can change if we always think positive and we free ourselves from the negative of our past. We are a light, but the light switch is in the mind and it is called "thought". When you are discouraged and sad, pick yourself up with this promise that the Eternal One made to you, " For I know the plans I have for you, says the Lord, plans to prosper you and not to harm you, plans to give you hope and a future."

What We Give, We Receive

This thought aligns perfectly with "The Golden Rule", "The Law of Attraction", "The Law of Sowing and Reaping", "The Law of Karma and Dharma", "The Law of Talion", "The Law of Life and Death" and the "Law of

Boomerang". All of these laws are expressed in different ways but come to the same conclusion, that what men give, that is what they receive. This can be applied to the spiritual and emotional areas, as well as the romantic, and also the actions and thoughts.

While I was watching the movie "The Last Samurai", I noticed a countless number of teachings that it was projecting. One of the phrases that I wrote down was: "Life would not have any sense if there was no one to share its Light with." I have seen that many people have problems only because they focus their thoughts only on themselves instead of thinking of ways of helping others. There is no better therapy for a sick soul than to help others that are suffering from your same ill. Helping others releases good within ourselves.

I was raised in a home where field workers would come and stay with us as part of our family. Some weren't family, but my parents would treat them as if they were. Nothing bad ever happened to us and we never had a problem with someone paying us evil for good.

This was what enabled me to develop a naive trust for people and when I got married I did exactly what my parents had done. There was a time in the Dominican

Republic when we received so many people in our home that the immigration authorities came to investigate because we thought we had a business of undocumented immigrants. But if there is anything that I can vouch for, it is that we never lacked for anything. And although many have betrayed us, we have always been favored with people who helped us. People become disillusioned with other people and they withdraw into their pain, but withdrawing yourself to hate others is the worst condition.

People with thoughts of depression and bitterness are always thinking in the bad that life has handed them and the problems they have, as well as how useless they are, in the lack they have, or in what they have lost. All of this causes them to concentrate on their problem and they live in anguish more than what is normal. If such people would only focus in getting out and helping others, they would soon forget about their own problems and would realize that they have an inner Light that if they would only let it shine, others would appreciate them so much more. And the idea that everything that surrounds them is a world of darkness, would disappear.

Sing with someone, go out with someone, dance with someone, give someone a word of hope or comfort. If the time you spent at home thinking about all the bad in your life you would begin to spend in helping someone else, your life would change, because what you think about, you focus on.

This is the difference between life and death, that the living always have something to offer. But death is a complete darkness, because there is no state of awareness.

Once they asked Mother Teresa of Calcutta how could she treat others with so much love, and put her hands on the wounds of sick people without feeling disgust. She responded, "My Lord Jesus said: 'for what you did to one of my little ones, you did it to me.' Every time a see someone sick and wounded, I don't see him, I see Jesus." This concept is more than just doing something, it is more than just helping people.

Being aware of the fact that we are someone and we possess something good to give, that we are torchbearers of a greater Light, of a brightness that gives us a sense of identity that enables us to act over and above our limitations. Life is about being aware that we were created with the capacity to give something good, to have a purpose in life.

This is the difference between life and death, that the living always have something to offer. But death is a complete darkness, because there is no state of awareness. People who resign themselves to a state of mind below what they were created for are conformed to live in a state of death. If you think that you have nothing to give, you will think that you have no reason to live, and that life or death make no difference to you. We are light and light is not without but within.

I remember that in the first year of coming to the United States I was overcome by a terrible depression that turned into severed anxiety. I couldn't sleep and I had panic attacks, I almost slept underneath my wife. At times when I was traveling, I wanted to crash my car. I had many thoughts of suicide.

One day I stayed at home exercising a spiritual fast, asking God to remove the ghosts of my mind. When 15 days had gone by without eating, I called Andres, my first mentor. I was desperate and I needed a miracle. I couldn't see my way and in my mind was that thought of dying that wouldn't go away. It was like it was nailed to my mind and nothing could remove it.

I started talking with Andres and after asking a few

questions, he asked his children and his wife who were there with him, to leave the room. He knew that a spirit of depression had taken control of my mind and he knew that when he began to work with me it would affect his environment also.

That's how it is, friend. Depression, feelings of dying, thoughts of suicide, feelings of inferiority are vibrations and they into a contagious environment. When my friend dismissed his family from the room I became even more terrified; I wanted to hang up the phone and finish dying, but I didn't have anywhere to run. I would have to face the fact that something bad was inside of me, that I was not well and I needed to receive help from someone.

At that time I was working for an organization where fellow workers did not trust one another, where any type of rare manifestation was considered a demonic attack or insanity. This was the only person that I trusted enough to tell him what was happening to me, but I had tried for over a month to resolve my problem by myself. The idea that when I went to preach at some church I should have some kind of an attack tormented me more than the problem itself. Day and night that is all I thought about. I would tell myself, "I will lose credibility if something like this happens to me in public. If I faint, or scream out, or my voice suddenly changes…if anything like that were to happen, they will never let me minister again. I will have to resort to selling things on the street and I will have lost everything I fought so hard to obtain."

When he was alone he prayed for me which did little for the state I was in. But then he asked me two questions that changed my life. The first question he asked was, "What are you doing these days?" At that point I didn't have strength to even talk, hunger was killing me. But I got up the energy to say softly, "I am in a fast for more than 15 days." He said, "Stop fasting and go eat."

The second question he asked me was, "Are you doing something for others?" "No," I replied. "I feel miserable and am scared that something will happen on the road or in someone's house." He said, "Get out of the house and go help someone else and you will see that they are in worse condition than you are."

I went out right away and began visiting people in their houses, offered my help and prayers, and before I knew it, my issues began to disappear. The thoughts of suicide, depression and the horrible anxiety attacks disappeared.

To understand why my problems left me, you'd have to

understand why they came. At that time I was immersed in my growth, personally and financially. I went wherever they invited me, besides my responsibilities as pastor of two churches, I kept up two radio programs, I went to other places evangelizing, and at times I would preach three and four times in one day when invited by other churches. Several hours a week I would help the son of a doctor who had problems with his nerves. I would try to find promotional announcements for one of my radio programs that was not being funded sufficiently by listener donations. I wrote, read, took care of the parishioners, took some classes to learn English, and accepted requests for interviews, and took care of my two small sons, getting their milk for them when they woke up in the middle of the night.

Besides all of that, my daughter, Wesserline, suffered from frequent nightmares and many nights I had to spend the whole night trying to get her to sleep. I also had to endure the emotional changes that my wife was suffering from postpartum depression. I would leave when no one else was up yet and got back when everyone had gone to bed. I was only concerned about being a good provider for my family and how to make a difference in this country.

One night, after arriving home late, my wife started to

fight, and to make demands; I shouted at her and said some hurtful things. She broke into tears, her hands bent back and her face transformed and she passed out for a moment... fear and guilt invaded me to the point that I was losing control. That night I took care of her and took her to the doctor and though she came around and felt better, I did not. I did not want her to remember what had happened. I had been working on my best psychological tricks to divert her attention so she would not find out the truth about what happened. Neither did I tell her what was going on in me because I did not want her to get sick and that is how everything started.

After talking with my friend, I decided for the time being to stop the radio programs, avoid the interviews, stop accepting invitations for conferences, and just dedicate my time to visit people at home and spend time with my family. I would take my wife where her family lived, visit long lost friends, and help where I could. Many times when I was in someone's house, I felt like I couldn't take any more and that I would pass out. Sometimes I couldn't take any more and would have to excuse myself and leave, but I kept doing it until everything disappeared.

When I finally healed, I went on vacation with my wife and my children to the Dominican Republic for 21 days and the rest is history. Nowadays I can do many things, but I never forget those principles that I learned during those difficult times. I always find time to visit some friend; I always find time for my family and I always try to help someone who needs something from me. To me, this is what is most important.

> *"Freely you have received, freely give."*

Many times when I participate in a radio or television program, people with problems call in and ask how they can receive my services; they tell me their need for spiritual or emotional help and I make an appointment with them. Then when they ask how much I'm going to charge them, I tell them that my pay is that they go and do the same for someone else. "Freely you have received, freely give."

This dear reader, may sound foolish, but it is powerful medicine for the soul: become concerned for others beginning with those who are closest to you because this can change your life. Your thoughts will be distracted from dwelling on your problems and allow you to think more about solutions.

I conclude this chapter by saying: "Man gives what he

has and has what he thinks." No more, no less. Man is a Light, but this Light turns on when he thinks positively and doesn't focus only on the problems. Every person, no matter who that may be, when they feel like they are living in darkness, needs to change his way of thinking and if he does this his life will change.

The Power of Light

Chapter 6

The Energy of the Word

We have already established that we humans are charged with light and that we are a source of energy. Because man was created in the image of the Creator, we could say that the essence of God is energy and this is one of the reasons why everything that he has made is charged with energy.

It is said that a human being could have more energy than is needed to light up a whole city, because not only does man have energy in all of his body, but he also generates energy. This is important to understand because this is the basis for the power of God, the power of the universe and the power of man.

There are times when I rub an object with my body and

a spark of lightning is emitted. This happens because a charge of energy has been produced. This charge in a much greater power can be observed when clouds rubbing together produce lightning bolts that are capable of killing a person or animal.

Vibrations are produced when energy moves in an environment and it can produce changes or tensions.

Energy has the power of sustaining the world but also the power to make it disappear. With an atomic bomb one could destroy the world. Richard Feynman said, "There is enough energy in one cubic meter of space to boil all the oceans of the world."

In this introduction I am talking about physical energy that can be felt in the heart, in the body, in the brain and in different organs of the body. This same energy is evident in space, and in the immense and powerful universe.

But there is an energy that goes way beyond the comprehension of many, and that is the energy of vibrations. Vibrations are produced when energy moves in an environment and it can produce changes or tensions.

Starting from this simple explanation, I say that when we talk about this energy, the vibration energy, we are talking about powers that can change the environment and came make things pleasant or unpleasant.

Spirits produce vibrations. This may not sound scientific, but it is not my intention to make it that. I say it because I believe there are powers and occult laws that govern the universe and there are also occult spirits that move about in the universe. These live in a different dimension to ours and they only appear when they are invoked, by faith and the vibrations of the emotions, thoughts and words.

When you feel an emotion, be it positive or negative, this not only affects you but also the people around you. So then, if my emotions can affect other people, that means that these are something more than a sound that comes from within, they also manifest themselves.

I once met a young lady in Dallas, Texas. She came to talk to me after a conference about how depressed she was and how she felt for all of the different conflicts that she was going through. From the moment she came to me I felt a deep sadness and an overwhelming sense of tiredness. She had not even spoken to me, had not begun to tell me her problems, but I already felt the weight of them. This person had a spirit of depression that was causing all of the energy around her to be bad, and making other people around her be affected by that negative energy.

Why am I speaking about this when I should be speaking about words? Because if we believe that words have power and these can produce things, we have to understand where this power comes from and what is the reason that words are more than just letters and sounds. You need to understand that these not only cause vibrations but they can change the vibrations. What I am saying is that words can change your destiny forever.

Words Are Spirit

This means that they are more than sounds and that they act hidden from sight. They work in another dimension. I have heard scientists talk about the possibility that there is another world parallel to our own. I have no doubt about this scientific theory. I know there are other physical worlds and understand there are also other spiritual worlds. Words act in both worlds. Jesus taught the people who listened to Him about the power that words have when He said, "...the words that I have spoken to you are spirit and life." He is not saying that they give life or that they have life, but that they are life, that that is what they are.

Number one: Words are a spirit. What is a spirit? Spirit is a hidden force. This force is manifested through energy, vibrations, words and emotions. Why? Because spirits cannot be see by human eyes. This force can manifest itself in a positive manner, like a fount of goodness and love.

God, for example. "God is spirit; and those who worship him must do so in spirit and in truth." What this means is that we can only feel His vibrations, His goodness and His miracles, His love, His power and His manifestations, but never His body or His flesh because he has none. God can bring everything spiritual to the natural, from the invisible world to the visible, but in essence that is not natural, nor is it flesh or blood.

Demons also are spirit and their manifestations are similar, but they are a negative force. Many believers blame Satan for all the evil that happens, but they forget that they can't assign blame to a spirit for anything, in view of the fact that a spirit in and of itself, does not have physical power, or physical life, and cannot manifest itself in the physical world unless it is given that ability by those that enable it to manifest itself.

An example of this is God, who is all-powerful, but does not manifest Himself in the natural except through faith. God is love, but He will not help your marriage unless you let Him into your life.

This is the principle on which to base all answers to questions posed by men and women such as, "Why do so many people die in wars? Why did so many people die in the Twin Towers catastrophe of 9/11 in New York? Where was God when this or the other happened?

He is spiritual and He will always act in the spiritual realm. He will only manifest Himself in the natural world with the help of man, who happens to be the designated being the He assigned to live and reign in the natural, physical realm.

If this is true about God, who created everything and established the existing laws that govern the universe, how much more does this apply to the spirit of darkness. That spirit cannot do anything evil against you except with your permission. And that permission is only granted in the spiritual realm. Just as there are spiritual forces that move God, so there are spiritual forces that move Satan and the spirit realm of darkness. "For our struggle is not against flesh and blood, but against the rulers, against the authorities, against the power of the dark world, and against the spiritual forces of evil in the heavenly realms."

My belief is that there are forces that move in the darkness and others in the light. But when we talk about the forces that were created by God to manifest His good, these depend on how man uses them because these forces have the power to penetrate the light as well as the darkness.

I don't have the time to explain this and neither is it my intention to give you a course on Theology. What I want you to understand is that there are spiritual forces and there are spirits that take use those forces for their advantage. Whatever you call those spirits doesn't change the fact that they exist.

Number two: Words are life and they are alive, and if they are alive, they move, they reproduce and they have energy, due to the fact that anything that is living has energy. Due to the fact that words are "spirit life" they have a purpose and a level of conscience. That is why when a word leaves a mouth it produces an effect for good or evil, for life or death, for blessing or curse.

When a word is spoken, the spirit that accompanies that word will see to it that that word accomplishes it's purpose. That is why a curse or a blessing what was spoken over you or someone else can be canceled by another word of greater force or magnitude.

Great Leaders Have Believed This

If I begin to mention the names of men who throughout history used their words to achieve their purpose, for sure this book would not be able to hold them all. That is why I will only mention some of their names and the most well known in present day context. These great men first conquered themselves and their own mouths, before winning others.

All of those people who remain registered in history as liberators or promoters of a better world, focused their words on the positive, on love and peace, but we cannot ignore or deny the fact that many used their words to incite violence, hatred, racism, etc. and they had a country free of any power to be able to subject it to the bondage of slavery from which it had emerged. Many leaders who simply used their words to obtain a change of government later found themselves implicated

> *When a word is spoken, the spirit that accompanies that word will see to it that that word accomplishes it's purpose.*

in a sequence of a coup, assassinations and death, because the dead cannot give life, only the living have power over the dead.

The mouth has power and it must be used for the growth and well-being of others. Martin Luther Kind, who was the Nobel Peace Prize and was a great defender of human rights in the United States, understood how much power words have when he said, "Nothing is forgotten slower than an offense…"

The problem of an offense is not in the offense itself, but in the word that accompanies it. I remember that I loaned $50,000 to a warehouse manager who had me convinced he was my friend. Every month he was to pay me a certain amount until he had paid me back, with a minimal charge of interest, but after three months, he stopped paying. After a year of trying to resolve the issue, conversation ended and the worst of it all is that I discovered that not only was he not interested in paying me back, but he was also an inconsiderate fraudster.

He said to me, "You are a thief, because all pastors are thieves!" I had not only trusted this man with a large sum of money, and even though he was not keeping up with his side of the deal in making the monthly payments, I was counseling his daughters and his wife. In other words, we still treated one another as family. The issue of money had not been a reason to cause a separation between us.

But the moment he said that to me, along with the death threat that me made me, we separated forever. The offense that came out of his mouth had more power than the amount of the debt or the delinquent fulfillment of the agreement.

In all that we do, this premise is a reality: words have more power than matter. Jesus said, "Because you have so little faith, I tell you the truth, if you had faith as small as a mustard seed, you can say to this mountain, 'move from here to there' and it will move." The word that comes out of the mouth comes out with the power to move matter. This allows us to say that in the world of the supernatural, the problem is not matter, but rather the man of little faith that stops before it. For the man who knows the power that is in his mouth, it does not exist.

The Light of a man who wants to be a leader is that he knows what he wants and his words are aligned to that purpose. No man is greater than another. The difference between one man and another man is the level of belief and the words they use.

Mahatma Gandhi said, "Usually, a persons becomes what he believes he is. If I keep telling myself that I cannot do something, it's possible that I will end up being unable to do it."

The greatest leader of the Hebrew people was Moses. He was elected by the "I Am" to free the nation of Israel from 400 years of slavery. The account says that when the great "I Am" presented himself, Moses began to complain that he didn't know how to speak, and that disqualified him for the task. Moses knew how important it was for a good leader to be able use of the power of speech, but what he did not know then that the Lord knew, was that the power of words is not exactly in the ability of the person, though these do have their effect, but in the beliefs of the person.

No words have power to make a lasting change unless they are based on an inner conviction. Most of the story of the call of Moses is about God trying to convince him that he was the right man for the job. In this attempt, the Lord used Moses' rod, which was the instrument to convince him that He would be with Moses to overcome the Egyptians. But as the story unfolds, we see that Moses' battle was not against the Egyptians but against his own people, who constantly complained about having left Egypt.

That is why I would argue that although the instrument of supernatural power that God gave Moses was represented with a stick, the struggle Moses had was not with that but with his words. All of his time of leading Israel was using his words for life or death, blessing or cursing. With these he survived a rebellious people, with whom he had to deal with for 40 years and with his words overcame all of the obstacles in the desert.

The greatest leader that the world has had was Jesus, and I'm not just saying that—look at His accomplishments and the number of His followers. Born in a tiny insignificant part of the Roman Empire, then we add the fact that he was not even of the government elite of that nation, much less did he even have their support. Nonetheless,

His words and His vision had such a deep and profound impact on His disciples that today His teaching has the most followers in the world. His convictions were what gave power to His words. He declared himself as "The Light of Life" "The Light of the World", "The Resurrection and the Life" and "The Salt of the Earth."

His story says that one day he stood in front of a tomb of a person who had been dead for 4 days and called out to the dead corpse: "Lazarus, come out!" The studious of the sacred texts say that the reason Jesus included the name of Lazarus was because of the incredible power of His words; if He had not said the specific name of Lazarus, all of the dead would have resurrected.

You could deny this fact, but no one can deny that His disciples were so convinced of His power that they followed His example. To them He said, "Everything that you ask in prayer, if you believe it, you will receive it."

In the dark times of religion and tyranny, the conviction of this power was lost, and Christians became people who believed certain doctrines but not with true conviction.

Today God has been revealing this power that had been hidden in the belly of the monster called "religion" and those who understand that God's desire for their children is a better world are accepting and practicing the power of words. I firmly believe that through this power we are going to see once again resurrection of the dead, healing of the sick and many will not see death as happened to Enoch and Elijah. The power of God is in your mouth and you can be a man or a woman who immortalizes yourself for eternity and history if you start using it.

The Power of Life and Death

"The tongue has the power of life and death…" At the "Palabras de Vida Church (Words of Life Church)," in Bronx, New York, I met a speaker who spoke on the topic, "The Third Day." During his message he told us his personal story, which caught my attention and I decided to include it in this teaching.

When he was 12 years old he was included in the football team at his school. Because he played well, people thought he would do an outstanding job. Here is what he said about his life experience at that age.

When I became a part of the team everyone had a nickname. One guy they called, "Rambo," another, "Pelé," etc. As soon as they saw me, they started calling me "Memín." Everybody forgot my real name and began to call me, "Memín." It spread like wildfire.

"At first I was proud because I thought that name was given because of my abilities. "Memín" must be a very famous person, and it was true. "Memín" was very famous, but the name wasn't given to me because of the fame of "Memín" but because of how ugly he was. If you've never seen "Memín" you need to Google it and then you will know what I'm talking about.

I don't know what happened, but from the moment I found out the ugly truth about "Memín" I began to live with my head down, a low self-esteem, and no self-worth. My body kept growing and so did my problems. An overwhelming depression took hold of my being.

I began to believe that I was really "Memín" and I couldn't change that name. The name personified me. People would call me by that name—old friends as well as new ones—they thought it was funny.

One day I noticed a cute girl and the thought entered my head that I had as much right as anyone to fall in love. So I got up my courage and asked her to go out with me. Her answer surprised me. Immediately she said, "Of course,

Memín!" So I asked her what restaurant she wanted me to take her to. She said, "No, come to my house Saturday at 7 pm, no one will be home." "Fantastic!" I said. I couldn't believe my luck!

On Saturday I dressed up and I went to the girl's house. At seven o'clock I was knocking at the door. I rang the doorbell but no one answered. I rang the doorbell again and again, but in the end no one came to open the door. It was then when I realized the meaning of her answer, "Come at 7 pm… no one will be home." She played me for a fool—she never intended to go out with me! I should have known it was too good to be true.

From that day on, my inferiority complex became acute. The embarrassment that I felt, the frustration of being made fun of, and my friends who kept calling me "Memín," was unbearable. It all culminated in me deciding to take my life.

Because my father was a pastor and almost every day of the week he had church services, I decided to do it on Thursday night alone in my room, because that was the night there were no activities.

Thursday came and my plans were in place, but something

unexpectedly happened. A preacher came to town, and my father decided to hold a church service that night. He called all of the parishioners and informed them that there would be a special service that night. So I decided to carry out my plan after the service. Sooner or later, it didn't really matter.

I arrived at church and as always, sat in the middle—I had a complex about sitting in the back and my self-esteem was too low to sit near the front. I always sat in the middle because there, I knew no one would notice me.

The preacher began, and I got sleepy. He was boring and tiring, but then he said something that made me lift my head. "When a man is intimate with his wife, he deposits within her millions of sperms and when this happens, all of them race to reach the ovary first. But only one makes it, and that one is you." The preacher pointed his finger at me. I was surprised to hear someone talking about sex in church, but what really shocked me was of all those attending the service, the preacher pointed directly at me. He didn't take his eyes off of me and continued, "You! You that feels useless, think you're ugly and have an inferiority complex, I want to tell you that God created you to be a winner. Out of all the others, you came in first. In other words, even before you were born you were a winner."

Those words woke me up and shook me up. Yes, I was that person, with a purpose. I was not just surplus in the world. I was never a failure! Before I was born I had already participated in a marathon, and I had won! I fought against all the rest of the sperm and I made it first, and when I made it there, I broke the egg with my strength, and I became a living being.

From that moment on, I decided to see the good in life. I got up and decided to keep living. When I showed up at school my friends called me "Memín" again, but I made it clear what was my real name and what they should call me from now on. I had a good name and they had to respect it."

As I write this book, I decided to tell this story because it has a great lesson, and it relates to what I am talking about. The power of words and the power that words have to give life or death. When they made this young man feel that he wasn't worth anything, when they told him he was ugly, when they used derogatory words against him, he started to die.

But when he received a word that gave meaning to his existence, he got up with the strength of a buffalo. I listened to him for an hour and a half. I really saw his talent, but all that talent could have died if someone hadn't point it out and told him the opposite of what he had thought of himself.

The power of life or death is in your mouth. But I ask you, "How many people have your words killed, beginning with yourself?"

In the story of Exodus, when the people of Israel left Egypt to the land that God had promised them, it has been estimated there were about three million people. To make it to the Promised Land they had to cross a great desert. Every one was very happy, dancing and singing, until they had to face their first obstacle. Then they started to complain, saying, "Why did you bring us out of Egypt to this terrible place? It has no grains or figs, grapevines or pomegranates. And there is no water to drink. We wish we'd died with our brothers before Jehovah. Why did you bring us here to die with our animals?"

That day, the Israelites declared their destiny. Everyone older than 20 years old died, except two, Joshua and Caleb. They had a different mentality. When everybody else saw the obstacles and the enemies, cursing themselves saying, "We know we are going to die here, we won't be able to reach Jordan." But Caleb silenced the people before

Moses and said, "...let's go up quick and take possession of the land, for we can certainty do it." This is the power of words. You can say this makes no sense, but it's true because there are thousands of examples like the one I gave you. People have lived because of words, and others have died because of words.

Another example of the power of words is that of Benson Idahosa, who had so much power in his mouth, that dead were raised and everything that he said was fulfilled. His death was a bit strange and even senseless. One day, when he was with a friend, he said, "Whoever drinks this Coca-Cola will drop dead." He drank it and died. The tongue has the power to kill or to give life. If you start complaining about what you don't have, if you say degrading things about yourself and others, that is what you will have. Avoid words that bring death, focus on saying all the words that full of life.

Words Feed Your Purpose

The question you need to ask yourself is, "What is my purpose?" Purpose is the pretension or intention of something we want to achieve. When I say that words feed your purpose, I am referring to this fact. People attempt many things in life, but on the way they give up and abandon that attempt—they abort their purpose for living. Why? Because the mind attacks that purpose with limiting beliefs of the sub-conscious. I have seen this time and time again.

When I was attending university, I met Victor and Maria. Victor came from a low-income family and she had been raised in a home for orphans that was only a few kilometers from the university. Both went to university trying to achieve a better future. But to start

> *The tongue has the power to kill or to give life. If you start complaining about what you don't have, if you say degrading things about yourself and others, that is what you will have.*

with, they had to work at the university as "industrials", which was the term the university gave to those who had to pay for their tuition by working at the university for one year. She worked in the laundry facility, and he in the bakery. There they met, started talking and soon fell in love.

When their work-year ended, they began to study their first year of studies in the university and completed it. He was studying to be a psychologist, and she to be a teacher. We became good friends because together we had gone to the same process to start out career at the university. But the following summer we went to the city of Santiago as book salesmen. The purpose was to make enough money during the three months of summer vacation to pay for the next year of studies at the university, and that way avoid having to work as "industrials" again, or have to miss classes because of a lack of money.

Victor was so head-over-heels about Maria, he had no interest in working very hard. The only thing they could think about was spending time together and they began to put up excuses that losers give when they are faced with some commitment. "But we don't know how to sell... this is not our style... this is too hard... this is really an injustice... its just not worth it to work so hard for others to live well at our expense... many professionals don't even have a job... etc."

When summer ended they couldn't go back to classes. When I was about to start my next semester I saw Victor in the registrar's office; he was devastated and bitter. He couldn't understand why after having worked so hard his first year in order to start university, he could not continue his studies. I encouraged him to continue, and told him he shouldn't quit his studies, but instead, work again for another year for the university; that's what I would do.

But Victor said he would stay in the city of Santiago, because he and Maria had other plans. And true, they did...I heard later that Maria was pregnant.

I never saw them again, and they didn't continue their studies at the university, that had cost them so much in the beginning. Why? Because what you focus your attention on is what you talk about, and what you talk about becomes the source of your creation. Victor did everything possible to begin his studies, as long as he was not in love with Maria. But once he fell in love he focused his attention on her and did not value anything else around him or anything else he did. Why? Because he felt that everything else distanced him from the woman he loved. And she, having been raised as an orphan with no one to really love her, clung to Victor, afraid to lose him, and convinced him to marry her before he did anything else.

When people no longer want to do something, they do two things. The first thing they do is criticize and look for reasons to justify themselves for not doing what they should be doing. The second is to lack the power to achieve it because every time they open their mouth, the only talk of their frustration with life. Talk about what you want and not about what you don't want.

People complain all day about what they can't achieve or accomplish. They complain about their limitations and the little possibility of doing something, but this will not help them to achieve what they so long for. No one has ever gone far by complaining. Complaints don't resolve problems, on the contrary, they only make them worse. Every day from the beginning of dawn speak to what you want. Say, "I am fortunate; I am blessed; I live a good life; I don't have debts; money is mine in abundance; I am good at getting money; everything that comes to me, prospers; everything I touch, multiplies; I have a great marriage; I have great children; I have a father who loves me; my God prepared everything for me even before I was born; nobody can stop me because He is watching over me, and protects me from mine enemies; no one can deceive me; I am happy; I live in abundance; I have a healthy body."

Declaring the goodness of God to you is the key to live a better life. You need to learn to declare words of good and not bad. When you focus on the problems, you will talk of them and you will attract them to you with the power of your mouth. Daily, I see people who begin to complain and curse at the first sign of some difficulty. They grumble about life and they lament all the time their bad luck or their lack of opportunities. But what they don't realize is that they are attracting to themselves more of the same by the power of their mouth. What you invoke, talk about, or curse, will happen.

When I am at the gym I take advantage of declaring words of good over every person I know. I speak to their life and I bless them. This seems like something

Complaints don't resolve problems, on the contrary, they only make them worse.

tedious but necessary. First, I start declaring that their lives are going to be greatly blessed and they are going to do well in everything they do.

Second, I declare over them and binding with my spirit. I do this mentioning their name and saying, "Mr. or Mrs. X, I love you or I forgive you? This has been the means of greatly improving my relationships, but it has also benefited in their improved treatment of me.

But you may say, "Wilson, this doesn't make sense. Why do you say that this will improve a relationship with someone who is not even present when you speak to them?" Because when I improve, everyone improves; when I love, everyone loves. My relationships improve because I am speaking to my inner man and I am telling my subconscious that I need to love, forgive, accept that person, but also, I am saying that I am responsible for any problem that there might be in the relationship.

Another reason why the relationship begins to change or strengthen is because words are spiritual and in declaring those words, the spiritual world assumes responsibility of making happen what I am declaring. They don't need to be there because God and I are witnesses and He will make sure that what I declare, happens.

In this chapter, my objective has been to take you to a level of perception where the words that come out of your mouth are conscious statements, knowing that your words have the power of light and darkness, of life and death, of blessing or evil.

There is a power in your mouth and you need to learn how to use it. The power is already in you. The Creator put it there. You can decide not to do anything, keep talking as you always have or you can begin to live an intentional life, declaring what you really want to have the life that you so much desire. "For the word of God is living and active. Sharper than any double edge sword, it penetrates even to dividing soul and spirit, joints and marrows; it judges the thoughts and attitudes of the heart."

Chapter 7

The Energy That
Exhales Life

Words come out of the mouth, but they are not produced there, rather, they originate in the depths of the heart. The most important thing about this power is that it's the energy that gave existence to everything.

In the story of creation of the lineage of Adam it says the following, "The Lord God formed the man from the dust of the ground and breathed into his nostrils the breath of life, and the man became a living being." Because all creation was made with the power of the word, man could not be an exception. Theologically speaking, the fact that the story says, "He formed," is the reason why many people think that man was not created by words but rather by the hands of God. They think that with His hands he made a figure of clay, and then He breathed the breath of life, which made him a living being.

I don't mean to contradict any tradition, but for us to be able to grow in the world of knowledge, it is necessary to know the truth, and that truth gives us the freedom to operate in a world of great powers, such as the word. Words are a world of magic. You can use magic as black magic, to curse, to criticize or to declare evil against someone (criticism, gossip and slander). Words are magic, but if you speak them to instill fear, judge others or rob them of their talent, their freedom, or their initiatives, you are manipulating them for your own interests. Your magic becomes black magic. Every word of evil is black magic.

Exhale With the Power of Your Mouth

Because the Eternal did everything with the power of words, we should know that the word "exhale" or "blow" is another way to say, "declare." I think this is something symbolic, or maybe an allegory of the writer Moses to take care and hide the word that God declared in this master creation. In this way, this knowledge would not fall into the hands of man but would remain in the mind of the Infinite.

Why do I say this? Because the same breath of life that man has, the animals also have, referring to life itself. But in regards to man, he was made in the likeness and image of God, and he was given a conscience, understanding and a soul when he was created, and thus there is a difference between man and an animal. If the breath that was put in the man when he was clay was the same spirit of life that the animals have, it would mean that the likeness of man was not the likeness of God, but rather the likeness of the animals.

For that reason I say that the word "breathed" is referring to a special declaration made over man, and that is why the writer says, "God breathed in his nostrils breath of life."

Throughout the story of the creation the same source was used, "the word." But unlike the rest of the creation, man has a mind like God's mind. This knowledge is what Moses called, "breath of life", and is the same as saying, "divine conscience." In other words, this account has nothing to do with exhaling literal breath, a *ruash.*

Many think it is just a wind, but the Greeks never considered it as a wind but rather as an identity, a source of inner knowledge and wisdom. The word "breathed" is talking about a spirit and that spirit exhaled is what we could call, "spoken word." Jesus said as much when he declared, "The words that I have spoken to you are spirit and they are life."

The Expression of an Invisible World

Words are spirit, in other words, they are the expression of the power, the conscience, knowledge, being and mind. They are the expression of a God that is in each man.

When a person speaks, his words are not limited to a simple sound. They are also a level of knowledge and conscience that releases what he wants to create or what is creating in life. What you are creating is what is expressed in the exhaling of your mouth, regardless of what you are creating: sadness, joy, loneliness, fortune, defeat, bankruptcy, happiness, love, wisdom, faith or uncertainty. In the end, all that you express or have expressed comes out by the exhaling of your mouth.

Moses, the first leader of the Israelites, wrote it this way, "...and He breathed in his nostril a breath of life... And the man became a living being." What can be translated as, "and the man became a conscious being." But, why is the term "in his nostril" used?

This term makes us think that life is breath that we can inhale and exhale through the nose. But this has nothing to do with it. In this context, the nose is symbolic because it is the organ that represents the means by which human beings inhale and exhale the oxygen that keeps the blood alive and the lungs working. What the term implies is an allegory of a deeper truth. The truth is that life or death is breathed into our interior. Jesus the Nazarene said it like this, "For out of the heart comes evil thoughts, murder, adultery, sexual immorality, theft, false testimony, slander."

This means that every word that enters our being becomes a concept, a belief, a virtue, a habit and wisdom. All of these, when formed by the power of the word that comes from the mouth of God, gives life, love, peace, health, happiness, empowerment and hope. All that comes out of the mouth of the Eternal One is good, pure and of good report. "The word of God is living and active." So that declaring a word of good to someone or something is to exhale life with the breath of your mouth. The person to whom it is declared will receive exactly as it was said. That is why I say that with the creation of man, the Infinite One declared an unknown word, that made man superior to the rest of all creation.

Exhale or Inhale With the Breath of Your Mouth

We have already learned that the Creator created all the things with the breath of His mouth. However, this is "... sharper than any double edge sword." It has a double edge because it is oriented in two directions: for good and for bad. Likewise, it's percussion is focused on a particular direction. People have the tendency to be what others say about them; that is the reason we can declare on people, people we love, and on the little ones, what we want them to be, because their formation has a lot to do with all that we declare for them to receive.

But this should not be this way. Every man should know who he is, and that within him there is a unique and superior conscience, and a resemblance to God. The Danish philosopher Søren Kierkegaard said, "If you name me, you deny me. Giving me a name, a label, you deny all the other possibilities that could exist. You classify one being to be only one thing, when you name it, when you arrange it. But at the same time, you are creating it, your define how it will exist."

We use words every day, and we cannot ignore the fact that they are always related to our destiny. While it is true that we use words to label people, we also use them to define and give them existence.

Giving a series of lectures in Fresno, California, a lady who was attending my conference in Reno, Nevada, eight months earlier, came up to me. Thanking me, she gave me a letter that she had in her hand.

The letter said, "God bless you. Millions of blessings to you and your beautiful family. Blessings for your gift and your profession. My name is Ana Galán *(her real name has been changed to protect her identity)* and I want to give you infinite thanks, because through your past conferences, I was freed from hurts that I was suffering since I was a little girl. Now I am a new woman. I am free! Thank to my God and to you who used His Word, I was able to rebuild and renew my life… I was born again! I have a life! I thank you with all my heart. I am now a very happy woman with many dreams, which become reasons to live. I appreciate you because of what you gave me; and I will always have you in my prayers. Much success, and thank you!

There are two important things in these declarations. First, by the way she speaks, is that she is a believer in God. Second, the conferences she attended were not religious conferences, they were not based on any creed, and I don't remember having any religious prayer, public or private, with this woman. I have never seen her, but she knew me, she remembered me, and she knew that in that event, that some religious people could even call mundane, I declared over her words of love and these did their proper work.

I didn't need to mention God for the words to have effect. I want you to understand this because it is not my intention to stir up a theological or religious controversy. What I am saying is that words in and of themselves have the substance of the one who created them and by possessing that substance, the results will be good ones because they are based on the original purpose.

When I speak at seminars I show people the power of the word and the power of self-suggestion. But, in contrast with some other speakers that stay in the theoretical, I like to call up someone from the public to demonstrate what I can do with my words. I begin with little things and move up to harder things until at the end they are asleep on the floor or doing some other thing that I ask of them. This scares some people because it sounds weird and beliefs have an impressive power to box people in.

This power is universal. It is a divine power given to man by God and it is only awaken by the knowledge that we are supernatural and spiritual beings. This power is activated with the renewed conscience of the divine within and it doesn't matter if I am in front of an audience invoking the name of God or not invoking any other name, but I just use the words and the results are always the same.

That is why God desires that the heart of man that is to make use of His gifts has a transformed mind, because these things in the hands of a selfish mind can be used to enslaved and deceive rather than bless.

The other thing that I can do is have people connect, know what their partners are thinking and can speak meaningful things into their lives, their purposes or their different situations.

This principle is taught by Jesus in the Gospel of John, chapter 14, verses 19 to 21. He said that we are all intertwined and that the thoughts and truths of the Father are in our thoughts and our words, and for that reason are in our minds. Knowing this, the only thing that I need to do when I go some place is to use that understanding. The understanding of who we are and what we possess is the main weapon to make things happen and to make that things we declare with our mouths become law and truth.

When I am in some place, I know that a light crosses the expanse of the universe to touch my head, and through that light, comes all the supernatural. But I understand that it will only manifest itself to mankind when I declare it. This is the power of the mouth, the power of life and death.

When I teach this in a particular place, those who are there and who believe operate under the same power as I. They begin to feel, experience and do things that they themselves are surprised they can do. This happens because the majority of people, though they have heard about the power of the mouth, don't believe and don't have the understanding that it is not about the mouth of somebody special, but it is in the mouth of everyone.

The Son of God, the Christ, gave us that level of conscience, and He demonstrated it to His followers by living in a world that exceeds human reasoning. He said to them, "…anyone who has faith will do what I have been doing. He will do even greater things than these."

Also in chapter 13 of the Gospel of John He says that

this power comes through the knowledge that He and His Father are one, and he who believes in Him, believes also in the Father. One of the problems that the normal reader has when reading these words of Jesus is that he sees Jesus as God speaking, forgetting that Jesus was a man. But a man who represented what a man should be, should live, should know and should do. In other words, the "image of the invisible God."

The first knowledge that Adam and Eve acquired from "the tree of the knowledge of the good and evil" caused man to live with a cloudy or darkened understanding. Man was put under the power of the curse, death, the laws of man, physics, matter and time.

That being true, theologically speaking, Jesus taught us how to live, speak and act as a "christ", which means "anointed". By accepting this level of knowledge and conscience we are accepting that we are as God, that we are seated in the heavenlies, that we have power over the grave and death, because the body is only a container and the divine knowledge of the eternal supersedes the temporal, because the eternal supersedes all limitations. The "I Am" is that knowledge. Knowing what is your place and know that there is no abyss that separates you from the being of

God, this is what makes you a superior being, a being that everything that your mouth declares will be fulfilled.

Remember, that knowledge can be, "You are a worm. You are nobody. There is nothing good in you," or you can focus on the truth, "I am, I am light, I am truth, I am blessing, I am liberation, I am love, I am peace, I am the image of the invisible God, I am a door, I am a connection between the natural and the supernatural. I am everything that is good, I am spirit, I am a miracle, I am a bridge to bring blessing, I am salt, I am a solution to the problems of humanity, I am the water of life, I am the hope, I am the possibility, I am the opportunity." And to this short list we could add to infinity and you can add your own. This knowledge is the truth.

Remember, words have two edges. We should not be surprised that there are so many people living in darkness and without hope; people who have decided to believe that they are nothing, thus declaring all kinds of curses over themselves, and over the world that is around them. If you chose the edge of darkness and lies, you will have death, but if you chose the edge of Light and truth, you will have life. It is easy to know what is truth and what is a lie. Everything that is against your greatness is a lie. Everything that propels you towards goodness is truth.

Chapter 8

Bitterness is Sinister and the Enemy of the Light

Bitterness is a dark feeling that deprives people from love and inner peace. It is caused by hatred; hatred of oneself, and hatred of others.

You may ask yourself, "Can a person hate himself?" Of course he can. Everything starts with acceptance or denial of oneself. Many people have lost because they haven't been able to leave behind grudges of the past.

I was watching the news on TV. They reported on a woman who killed her former teacher over the fact that when she was little, he had abused her. She grew up, got a degree, and killed him. Her sentence was 30 years in prison. Even though this woman had a career, she couldn't live her life; her inner pain, frustration and resentment wouldn't let her.

The Eternal One gave a commandment that has a lot to do with what I am talking about. This was revealed in all disciplines, philosophies and spiritual knowledge: "You will love your neighbor as yourself." We cannot overcome darkness with darkness, neither evil with evil.

The great human rights defender, Martin Luther King said, "If you give back hatred for hatred, hatred will multiply, add darkness to a night that is already lacking stars. Darkness cannot expel darkness, only light can do that. Hatred cannot end hatred, only love can do that." Love is the most lasting power in the world. This creative force, well exemplified in the life of Christ, is the powerful instrument available to humanity when searching for peace and security.

It is very important that we understand that every destructive feeling towards others is related to the lack of love; directed first toward ourselves, and then to others. No one can do anything for anybody if he doesn't first love himself. Bitterness starts with hatred towards others and or with the lack of self-esteem.

Forgiveness

Forgiveness covers three dimensions of life. The first is forgiving ourselves. The second is forgiving others, and the third is to know that our God has forgiven every wrong that we have done.

What is forgiveness? It is to free someone from an obligation or punishment; to forgive a debt. To give up a right, a pleasure, or enjoyment. To absolve, rescind, extend amnesty, dispense with, excuse, forget, exempt from, liberate, tolerate. It comes from the Hebrew word, *acad* which means, "the action of forgiving." It means to remit a debt, offense, fault, crime, or something similar. Remission of the sentence deserved, of the offense received or of some debt or obligation pending. The Greek word, *airo,* is a verb that means, take away, to carry, to put on oneself, to lift.

An example of this is that before Jesus came to this earth to fulfill his mission, He had a messenger whose name was John the Baptist. When he saw his master coming to the place where he was talking to the crowd, he said, "Look, the Lamb of God who takes away the sin of the world." The verb *"takes"* used in this affirmation is *"airo."*

Needless to say, people who think they have the right to take away the burden or blame of someone, are living an act of arrogance that comes from their ego, whereby the individual thinks he has been offended, and in a flamboyant gesture he absolves his offender. Forgiveness implies an offense. That is, if order for someone to be able to forgive, first there has to have been an offense. But because no one has the power to offend someone else, unless that person gives them the power to do so, it is paradoxical to note that pardon should never be about the person who supposedly offended us, but on oneself, for having given so much power to the offense.

Each person creates their own emotional state. In other words, people don't get upset about the cause of their problems but rather about the interpretation of the matter. The offender then, is always oneself: they offend you because you become offended. That is why I say that when a person forgives an offense the only thing he is doing is take the offense off himself to put it on someone else. This is the forgiveness he offers from God.

Many have misunderstood this belief and think that when God promises to forgive He is saying, "I am offended and I need a plea, for you to beg in order to forgive you." But quite the contrary, what He offers to His children is, "You hurt yourself, you offended yourself, you hurt someone else or hurt yourself, but I love you so much that I cannot bear to watch you bear your load, so give it to Me, I will assume the guilt, I will carry it on my shoulders, so that you can be free."

That is forgiveness: to take upon oneself with joy the offense of someone else in order that they not have to carry it any more. Forgiveness does not absolve the other person, but rather ourselves, because the intention is to assume the guilt as our own, carry it on our shoulders, assume total responsibility for our life and destiny, and stop suffering over the wrongs, mistakes and evil intentions of others.

To accept and love others as they are is what I call, "forgiveness." Only that way can we be free from the power of an offense, by taking it on our shoulders and accepting it as part of the errors of the past. And, because it is in the past, it cannot hurt our present. The words, "forgiveness" and "pardon" come from the Latin prefix *per* and the Latin verb *donaré* that when combined means, "pass, cross, ahead, pass over" and "donate, donation, gift, present, give."

I love the definition, "to pass over". First, because I believe that a person who cannot do that, cannot truly forgive. And second, I think that people who cannot forgive because of a problem of self-esteem, see themselves as inferior and they hate the person who they think has let them down in some way.

Forgiveness is a state of the conscience where people realize who they are and how insignificant hated, resentment and bitterness is towards someone or something. A woman whose husband cheated on her will live in frustration forever unless she works on her self-esteem. To many, the act itself is not as important as with whom it took place. If they perceive their opponent

> *People who cannot forgive need to work on their self-esteem, because they either feel inferior to the person who offended them or to the offense itself.*

as prettier, or if they think that their husband is a flirt that likes them all, they then will remain trapped in that emotion because they believe they cannot do any better. But the minute she realizes that these two with their affair did her a favor, be it because she found a better man or because she sees the brighter side of life, all negative emotion will be gone from her interior the day she realizes how important she is.

People who cannot forgive need to work on their self-esteem, because they either feel inferior to the person who offended them or to the offense itself.

This is the reason why I also believe that the offense has nothing to do with the act or the offender, but rather with the offended. The person who forgives needs to be able to renounce something that he has or believes is his right to own. For that reason, to be able to forgive, a soul needs to be well illuminated by the power of self.

Important Steps For Inner Peace

1.- Be aware of what happened.

2.- Be humanitarian.

3.- Show humbleness.

4.- Stay calm. Try this technique to deal with stress and to eliminate anger: breath a couple of times and think about something that gives you tranquility and peace, it can be an image that is related to nature or something else.

5.- Avoid waiting for an apology.

6.- Recognize the benefits of forgiveness.

7.- Forgive yourself.

One of the stories of the life of Jesus says that a handicap man was taken to him for healing. Jesus, instead of telling him, stand up and walk, he told him "...your sins are forgiven." With this, he was freeing him of all his past sins. Guilt can cloud inner peace, immobilizing people, and turning them into social handicaps, without success, with old ideas. They don't see how life can smile at them. They allow everything to perish and wither, letting themselves die because of the hatred they feel towards themselves and towards others.

The story tells us that the people around Jesus didn't understand why Jesus would say to the man, "Your sins are forgiven you." They were irate and reacted by accusing him, "Do you think you are God that you can say to this man, 'Your sins are forgiven you'?" Jesus answered and said to them, "That you may know that I not only say that I have that authority, but I will demonstrate it with this, I will tell the paralyzed man, "Walk!" And at that instant the man got up and walked, and everyone glorified God that He gives such authority to men.

This is the authority that a man or a woman can maintain in their soul when they realize they have nothing against anyone and that their Father God loves them more than anything else.

Forgiveness not only gives a man the authority to unchain himself, but to be able to help others do the same also. Those who surrounded the paralyzed man were forgetting a truth that the Master understood well, the power of forgiveness. When a person knows they have been forgiven, getting up will not take any effort. Every man and woman who lives in this world needs to know that in this instance Jesus did not exercise any power that you yourself do not have once you understand and experience this truth. The truth is that it is easier to get up from paralysis than forgive someone, because getting up is the result of a quiet heart full of inner peace.

Leave Your Backpack

Life is an uphill climb and we cannot advance with a backpack full of negative emotions. Many people prefer to walk that way and that is the reason why they shorten their life on earth.

Let me give you a list of emotions that can control you, until you decide to let them go: anger, depression, grudges, hatred, pride, mental illnesses, oppression, bitterness, resentment, etc. All of the above feelings are destructive, but the people who carry these emotions around, justify them.

My wife was quite bitter. When I married her I realized that I had married a woman that was very hard to please. We were not on the same page at all, and she did not like anything I did. Whenever we traveled she had an expression on her face of being mad, bothered, and she chewed gum all the time, hardly every smiling.

> *Negative emotions become internal forces that rob us of freedom and make us live prostrate before diseases and pain.*

It is hard to love a person who is mad or sad because everything they do, they do to justify their mood.

Time went by and I won't deny that there were some good times; we loved each other and we wanted to give our children then best and build a wonderful future together. But the bitterness in my wife's heart hindered her. She dragged that bitterness of a tragic experience she went through as a teenager.

When she was 14 years old, her father was unfaithful to her mother and not only that, but when her mother tried to rebuke him for it, he struck her in front of their kids. In that moment, the image she had of men was destroyed in her head, along with the image she had of her father. Even though in her mind she knew that she loved me, she could not love me like she wanted to, and without realizing it, she would attack me with all of her rage and anger. She was always in pain and her acne would not heal. I took out a life insurance and I assure you I believed I would need it.

Not until she had a personal encounter with God and His reality did my wife learn to love herself, love others, forgive her father, and along with him all other men. The moment she realized she had to forgive, those helping her through the process made her write out a list of the people she needed to forgive, tear up the paper while naming their names.

Though you may not believe it, when she did this she broke every band that bound her soul. She told me she couldn't do it; she couldn't tear up the paper nor mention the names. It was so hard for her she had a panic attack.

A bitter feeling within us brings a huge darkness that deprives us of seeing the true light of our soul and makes us slaves of our emotions. Negative emotions become internal forces that rob us of freedom and make us live prostrate before diseases and pain. They bind you with the painful events or people you hate so much.

Finally, my wife got free from all of those bad emotions. She gave her soul to God, and decided to live life to the fullest. This improved her appearance, literally, and she became another person, a woman more beautiful, sweeter, more attractive and interesting. I fell in love with my wife like never before, due to one reason alone, she was indeed another woman.

The mere fact of forgiving herself and forgiving those who she felt had failed her turned her into a positive person who always supports me and gives me encouragement in my projects. She stopped complaining about my job and began to appreciate the privilege that I do what I do. Before, she would complain about anything and everything; now she appreciates it, and says it all the time.

An act of forgiveness, to leave behind all these destructive emotions, can change you completely and turn you into a new person. It is possible that all of the problems you claim to have come from that. Even to the fact that nobody loves you or that nothing turns out good for you, can come from a bitterness of soul.

My advice to you is: Leave that backpack that is hanging on your soul and see how light life is and how illuminated is the way you can live. A person capable of forgiving radiates a light that attracts others and blesses everything that is close.

Bitterness Is The Fruit of Wounds

People suffer from different circumstances and situations in life, which are part of the growth and development of man. But bitter people don't know how to see the events as a part of life. Instead of seeing situations and circumstances, they see people. They make people responsible of their misfortune.

Bitterness can come from the following reasons: abuse at school, college, university, work, hurts caused in a relationships between parents and children, broken relationships between spouses, jealousy, failure to meet expectations that exist in the marriage, (economy, sex, loyalty), wounds when dating, broken commitments, etc.

I once met a young woman who couldn't stop lamenting the fact that she had married a man who cheated on her and took away all she had. She was a businesswoman in the city of New York. She developed a business that gave her millions of dollars in revenue. All of a sudden, she met a man from the Dominican Republic, they got married and started to travel around the world with the money she had accumulated.

She was happy and she was living a fulfilled life. She was

married, she had money, and she loved her husband. What else could she want from life?

But the unexpected happened. Her man got emotionally involved with another woman and when she reacted by taking away all of the money privileges she realized he was one step ahead of her…he had put everything in his name, he had emptied the bank account and had put it in his personal account.

Reality was hard for her, but she had to deal with it. She was alone, mocked, without a business, without money, without a husband, and in a country where she did not belong. She was a citizen of the United States so she decided to return home. But she returned full of pain and sadness.

Starting over was hard for her. Though she was a beautiful woman, she began to feel like no one would fall in love with her and besides, it wasn't worth living in a world of evil people. The pain was so acute, she could see no way out; her soul had been poisoned, she hated that man and everything to do with him.

Day after day the pain got worse. It got so bad she didn't think she could take any more. She couldn't sleep, she didn't eat, and a paralysis began to take hold of her body. The doctors did all kinds of studies and tests on her, but could find nothing wrong. Every day she got worse and worse in bed. Everyone would see her and expect the worse. Her tears had darkened the light of her world, hope and love. She couldn't stop crying day and night. A horrible thought of vengeance and suffering consumed her.

One day, laying in bed dying from the pain and desperation, she began to talk with God and tell Him that she was still young and did not want to die that way. She told Him about all of her troubles and what had happened to her and asked, if it were possible, to remove that bitter feeling in her soul.

In the middle of her conversation with God, a light surprised her; a powerful light filled the whole room. She couldn't get over such a phenomenon and didn't understand what was happening. But a voice spoke to her and said, "Get up! Because I love you, you will not die here. I am about to change your destiny."

Without thinking twice about it, she got up from the bed. She still couldn't figure out if the light was part of her pain, suffering, madness or a divine visitation. But she was in no condition to reason things through. As best she could, she stood up, left and building and began to walk down the freezing cold streets of New York city, in the dead of winter.

Looking like the walking-dead, dragging her bathrobe and still in her slippers, she didn't know where she was going or what she was doing outside her house, but she obeyed the voice that had spoken to her from the light in her room that had given her the strength to leave her bed. She walked like a zombie in complete silence and misery.

That was when an elderly gentleman who wanted to cross the street but upon seeing her said, "Maam, I need you to help me cross the street." She turned to see the man; he was quite elderly and walked with a cane. The first thing to come to her mind was, "I'm the one that needs someone to help me. I don't want to help anyone else." But she pushed aside that thought and paid attention to her protective woman instinct—she took the man by the hand and helped him get to the other side of the street.

The man looked at her, noticed her condition, took out his business card, and said, "Obviously you are not well, as a matter of fact, you look like someone who is near death. But God loves you and has a plan for your life. I have been waiting here for some time at this corner and I was asking myself, "What am I doing here?" And now I understand, you are the reason why I came her.

Before she could answer him he stroked his goatee with his hand, looked at her tenderly and said, "Call my secretary, make an appointment and we will meet in my office." The man with the cane was a millionaire doctor who lived in New York, who had retired and now dedicated his final days helping people who wanted to better themselves.

That Monday she went to the doctor's office who when he arrived sat down at his desk. She told him her story of why she was in that condition. He wrote her a check for $50,000 and gave it to her.

That day a new light of hope began to illumine her being. She left behind her past and dedicated herself to being a motivational singer. She was the one who introduced me to the world of motivation and personal transformation. She was an inspiration to my life—she was a light.

Bitterness always has a root, and only you have the power to remove it from your heart. The tools you need are the light of forgiveness and hope.

On Monday, the young lady arrived at the address of the business card. Indeed, the doctor was there as well.

Bitterness always will have a root that only you will be able take out; the tools to do it are the light of forgiveness and hope.

He entered his office, went to his desk and sat down to listen patiently the story of this lady, and the reason why she was in this condition. Without any hesitation he took a pen and wrote a check for fifty thousand dollars and gave it to her. Since that day, a new light of hope began to shine her being. She left her past behind, and dedicated her life to be a motivational singer. She was the person who introduced me to the world of motivation and personal transformation. She was the great inspiration to my life. She was the light. Bitterness always will have a root that only you will be able take out; the tools to do it are the light of forgiveness and hope.

Bitterness Causes Damage to All of Our Being

Bitterness not only makes us live in a world of emotional darkness, it also produces different kinds of damage. I will present at least thirteen of these:

1.- Bitterness can be seen in our conversations.

2.- Bitterness manifests itself in our relationships.

3.- Attitudes reflect in many ways if you are a bitter person or not, because your reactions are abrupt.

4.- Physical health can be affected by bitterness.

5.- When we are bitter, we hurt others.

6.- Bitter people build emotional walls to separate themselves from others in order to avoid being hurt again.

7.- Fear and mistrust can be the cause of bitterness.

8.- We are afraid that our inner hurts and our weaknesses be uncovered.

9.- Bitterness causes loneliness, because people isolate themselves.

10.- Bitterness always results in breaking up relationships.

11.- We push people from our lives because of the same attitudes.

12.- A bitter person assumes an attitude of complaining, pain and victimization.

13.- Bitterness steals your potential and doesn't let your light shine.

Types of Forgiveness

Psychologists and experts have made a division of forgiveness based on people's reactions when they are offended. The different kinds of forgiveness are: total forgiveness, partial, pure, conditional, expressed, implied, unexpressed, spontaneous and requested.

Partial Forgiveness – It is easy to forgive minor offenses, but difficult to forgive the ones that hurt us deeply. Once, a young lady interrupted a meeting in which I was speaking of forgiveness to assure me that someone who kills an innocent person should not be forgiven. I said, "I know how hard this sounds not only for yourself but for everyone here; but we must forgive everyone. Forgiveness does not mean that the person who committed the offense will not be punished under existing laws, but we will make sure not to load on more guilt or sentiment." We must not forgive just some of the offenses, but all.

Conditional Forgiveness – Then there are people who only forgive conditionally. They always express it in words like, "I forgive, but I never forget." "I forgive you, but remember what you did to me." "I swear, next time you will pay me for this." "Don't expect me to forgive you again." Or in the marriage relationship, "I forgive you, but we will not have any more intimacy," "I forgive you, but I need you to buy me a new car," "I forgive you, but get your mom out of the house," etc. When you condition your forgiveness instead of truly and unconditionally forgiving the other person, you are manipulating the situation and those dark sentiments will not diminish, but rather increase.

Genuine Forgiveness – This type of forgiveness is full and complete. The person offended lets go of all offense and all negative feeling that goes with it. This person knows that he is responsible for his life and his emotions. In order for a person to fill his soul with a forgiveness so pure, he needs to release others from their feelings and guilt, he needs to assume responsibility for what happens to him and stop blaming others.

Our Teacher Jesus taught this principle with His example, while he hung on the cross and was mocked and beaten by his executioners. Though dying on a cross what a vile, cruel and shameful way of dying, He never lost his composure nor His convictions. On the contrary, the account of his story tells it this way, "And Jesus said, 'Father, forgive them for they don't know what are they doing.' And they divided His clothing by casting lots." That is an act of greatness. I said earlier, that only a person who knows who he is, and has a strong posture of what he does and what he wants to achieve, can forgive. Forgiving is to let go of the offense and forget about it. In any case, it has to do with ourselves, assuming complete responsibility and ceasing to blame others.

> *The difference between a successful and an unsuccessful man is that the first one lets all the light out from his inner being, and the unsuccessful lets out all his frustrations.*

When I talk about taking responsibility for the offenses, I'm not talking about carrying an internal load of guilt feelings for everything bad we do or happens to us, but to accept that we are all intertwined and that we should accept that in one way or another, we are connected to each other.

When we think of a better world we are closer to achieving it. It has to do with letting go of those who want to hurt you and take responsibility for your own actions and life. This is a great act of humility. We can blame someone else and spend our entire lives full of frustration and misery or we can accept that everyone is innocent, and that what you have live in the past is past. The wrong that they did to you and the circumstances of life have nothing to do with those involved, but rather with the purpose that the Eternal One has for your life. He desires that your light shine bright.

Diamonds don't come out of a precious stone, they come out of pressed coal. Its beauty, its light and its value is obtain through the years and through a process. Gold comes from a rustic and ugly rock, which has to go through a process of fire for its brightness and splendor to show. The smelter knows that when he sees his face in the metal, it's the moment when silver has gotten its perfect gloss, at the same time, a lot of work and sand paper is needed for that to happen.

All these examples show us that many of the things you have been offended with are nothing but circumstances of life to get the riches and beauty and fullness out of your interior to the exterior. There is a great light in you, but it will never shine unless you get rid of what hinders you. The difference between a successful and an unsuccessful man is that the first one lets all the light out from his inner being, and the unsuccessful lets out all his frustrations.

I conclude this chapter by saying that forgiveness releases the hurts of the past. It allows you to get close to God and helps you to be happy and in peace with others and with yourself.

The Light That Enlightens Every Man

When we talk about "The light that enlightens every man", we are talking about a universal God that fills every man of knowledge and love.

Not long ago I was talking to someone about this, and he said to me: "But Wilson, the people do not like religions or religious messages"; to which I added that he was right, but that he should take into account a great truth that many want to ignore and that is that people in a very high level like you to talk to them about God, because there is a binding in the minds of every man with his Creator. The friend of Jesus, the beloved disciple John, wrote that the Word of God was what made it all come into existence when he said: "In the beginning was the Word, and the Word was with God and the Word was God"; and he expresses again: "That Word was the true light that enlightens every man coming into the world."

There is a superior light that enlightens every man and if he wants to be in this light he can live a supernatural life. When I speak of a supernatural lifestyle I'm talking about accomplishing and doing things that could not be explained by science, in laboratories or in the logic of the mind.

Many people deny the existence of God, since it cannot be tested in a laboratory, but 95% of everything that exists in the universe cannot be tested. How is it possible that people with such ignorance think they can prove the existence of God as Creator of such a vast universe?

I am among those who believe that none of us has enough knowledge of who God is. It would be impossible to think we have such knowledge. I think that the revelation that we have about Him is quite limited, yet I also know that we have enough revelation to believe in Him.

In my book, *More Than a Dream*, I say that God is manifested in all the goodness of man. But one thing is the manifestation of God and quite another is who He is. Also that every word that sounds in mind is not simply a word but a spiritual substance with power the of creating or destroying.

An example of what I mean is when you mention the words, hatred, bitterness, death, defeat, uselessness, depression, pain, clumsiness, etc., these words in their mere mention produce a bad vibration.

Similarly, when mentioning the words: love, kindness, happiness, wealth, abundance, health, light, peace, trust, these produce a positive vibration. The mere mention of good and nice produces that feeling, but again this is also the case when we mention the negative and destructive things.

If you think what I'm saying is a lie, try it with someone. Come up to someone and begin to speak with the emotion that you want to produce, and you will produce it.

I remember when I was little, I lived in an area where there was no TV and the nights were long and boring. Usually my grandfather was not at home, for during the day he was working the land and took care of his business at night. But there were some nights of the year he stayed at home and invited certain storytellers who were experts in mysterious things. I loved the stories from beyond the grave, but also they frightened me like a death row inmate. Often the stories followed me to bed and kept me awake. Other times, while they were still telling their stories and everyone was still up, I would sneak off to try to get to sleep before anyone else. Simply hearing those stories caused a terrifying feeling like living in a cemetery while watching the dead rise everywhere or like being in the middle of hell.

Words cause a sensation and affect our emotions and the results. That's why I want you to pay attention to what I'm telling you: words are not just words, but rather are the source and essence of the infinite God. And it is His maximum expression and essence of His power. "In the beginning was the Word, the Word was with God and the Word was God."

It has been demonstrated that words affect emotions and also affect the results. Words are the source of the supernatural. Words cannot be tested in a laboratory, but the results that are produced by words can be. In the same manner that God cannot be proven, it is the evidence of His creation through individual faith in the facts, that one can believe that He exists.

I heard a famous writer say that God is energy, because energy is the only thing that is in the past, the present and the future. And, energy is the only thing that transforms and does not destroy itself. When I heard that premise, I appreciated it and for a long time accepted it, but now I want to assure you that God is more than energy though He has energy. Not only is He energy, He is words, thoughts, substance, love, enthusiasm, happiness, health, life and liberation. God has energy but more He is more than that—He is a thinking, intelligent being, full of life.

Man, like God, is full of energy. But if man was only energy, scientists would have been able to resurrect the dead. Energy is something that is well known and it has been developed for multipurpose use. This example is very logical, in view of the fact that man is "in the image and likeness of God."

When life (God) leaves the body of a man, there is no energy that can raise him back to life. All of these components and thousands more that I could mention are what He is, because He is the source of power. God has the power of everything good and of life, "because there is one God and Father of all, who is over all and through all and in all."

Enthusiasm is a Supernatural Light

The word enthusiasm comes from the word formed of *"entheos"* or *"enthous"* (that has a god inside: *'en'* + *'theos'*) Enthusiasm means, "God in us."

It says that Jacob's spirit left him when he lost his son Joseph and it came back when he saw him again. Here is the story: "But when they told him everything Joseph had said to them, and when he saw the carts Joseph has sent to carry him back, the spirit of the father Jacob revived." Literally, this word means "came back to life."

Jacob had fallen into a great depression. Depression is a darkness that steals all the enthusiasm. Enthusiasm is a superior light that destroys all bitterness, depression, sadness and happiness. Enthusiasm is a divine entity. A person without God lacks enthusiasm.

When you see a person who has enthusiasm is because he is full of that superior light. But also, when you see a discouraged person, without enthusiasm, and depressed, it's because consciously or unconsciously he has died.

To enthuse yourself doesn't mean living, it means reviving. It means that life comes back, there is a resurrection, you are born again. People are not alive when they breathe and walk, but when they are happy, when they are enthusiastic. In other words, when they have God.

If you pay attention to what I am saying, you will see that I am not talking about a certain religion, but of a universal entity, because whether we want to accept it or not, God is light for all His children, and He shines over all men in the world, not only a few.

Some time ago I was invited to give a conference in Manhattan, New York. When I finished, a young lady came to talk with me. The moment she gave me her hand in greeting I noticed that she was under a great depression. She lacked strength in her hands, her smile was forced, her vibrations were very low and her posture displayed a lack of enthusiasm. She was not more than 20 years old, very attractive, but she lacked radiance. The lack of enthusiasm stole the light that her Creator had put in her. I began talking with her and asked why she felt so badly. She said it was because she didn't have anyone in this country, that she didn't like the job she had, that she felt along, sad and without any desire to live. While she was talking she didn't stop crying and it seemed like her sadness what going to overtake me too.

But when she finished telling me her story I looked at her intently and told her all the good that I saw in her, and what God was showing me for her future. She began to smile, and gradually, her face became radiant with every positive word she received, it was like turning a light on with a dimer switch, which gradually intensifies the brightness of the light.

In few minutes, this young lady became another person very different from what she was when she first came to talk to me. In the time I was assisting that organization, she was one of the best students that I had. She was talented, but her talents had never excelled because of the lack of enthusiasm.

The following is a list of things that you are. This list of qualities is something you can put at the head of your bed or on the mirror and read it every day. Once you start doing this you will begin growing in these areas. Reading them you will begin to transform your mind day by day, because that is where true transformation begins. If you can believe what you really are, instead of what others say about you, for sure you will be an enthusiastic person and a winner. One of the best ways to believe in what we are is to declare it every day.

Declarations

- I am who I am.
- I am salt of the earth.
- I am light of the world.
- I am a branch of the true vine and a channel of God.
- I am a friend of God.
- I am elected by God to take His fruit.
- I am a collaborator of justice.
- I am a son of God; God is my father.
- I am an heir, sharing inheritance with Him.
- I am temple and dwelling place of God; His spirit dwells within me.
- I am a spirit with God.
- I am a member of His body.
- I am a new creation.
- I am reconciled with God and I am a minister of reconciliation.
- I am one with God.
- I am an heir of God.
- I am holy.
- I am a superior creation to all of the others.
- I am a fellow citizen with the rest of the members of the family of God.
- I am just.

- I am a citizen of heaven, and I am sitting at the right hand of God.
- I am His favorite and hidden with Christ in God.
- I am the expression of life; the Father manifests himself in my existence.
- I am chosen by God for eternal purposes.
- I am loved by God.
- I am a son of Light; not of darkness.
- I am holy and a participant in the spiritual calling.
- I am one of the living stones of God, being edified by Christ as a spiritual house.
- I am a member of the chosen generation, a royal priesthood, a holy nation, a people chosen by God.
- I am an alien in this world where I am living temporarily.
- I am an enemy of evil, and I have power over it.
- I am born from God, and evil cannot touch me.
- I am health.
- I am abundance.
- I am peace.
- I am life.
- I am goodness.
- I am love.
- I am temperance.
- I am trust.

It is necessary that you repeat this list every day until you are completely renewed, until the Eternal has completed His masterpiece work in you for His glory!

The Light That Shines Your Path

"Jesus replied, 'A man who walks by day will not stumble, for he sees the light of this world; it is when he walks by night that he stumbles, for he has not light.'" We already stated that the light that shines is in every man, but this light manifests itself through the word, conscience, knowledge, enthusiasm, love, hope, and peace.

Now I would like to discuss one more aspect of light that has to do with wisdom. Wisdom is that inner voice that tells you to make good decisions and that permits you to judge with justice between one matter and another. We could also call "wisdom" the capacity to make things work efficiently. Wise people don't fail because they have a superior voice in their inner being that helps them to make right decisions, at the right time. Those who have wisdom know what advice to give, when and why to give it.

Wisdom is a higher light, but it is impossible to be wise unless we listen to our inner man. That is why wisdom is not base on learned knowledge, due to the fact that everything is in constant change and nothing stays the same. This has to do with following that voice that speaks from the depths of your inner being. Regarding your business, in your organization, and in all that you do, you need to learn to manage them wisely. Many people live in the past because they are not guided by wisdom.

A university professor who teaches classes on economy cannot guarantee that his students will turn out as prosperous individuals, because this does not depend on knowledge acquired in a university, but rather in the ability to make good business and economic decisions in every aspect of life. This is what I call, "wisdom".

Some years ago I had $70,000 that I kept in a safe-vault because I did not want to put it in the bank. My problem was that I was not a businessman, at least at that time in my life I wasn't. My focus in life was church, speak at conferences, and develop radio programs. In that quest to figure out what to do with the money, I called a lady who had sold me a life insurance policy because, according to her, her company also handled investments. But her reply was that she felt the amount was too large for her company to invest because she felt she did not have enough experience. She assured me that she would find someone who could do it. But that never happencd.

In one occasion, I stopped to talk to a "friend". He told me that he had been denied a loan that he had requested from a bank. I asked him why he wanted a loan. He told me he wanted to expand his business, and said that if I wanted, I could become his partner. I saw this as a great opportunity, and we agreed to look for $50,000.

During the time of the transaction I had an uneasy feeling within; everything posed difficulties. What I want to make clear is that a voice in my inner man spoke negatively about this business. It would speak to me while I was driving my car, and I had negative dreams about the investment. But because I had committed already to doing this business I silenced that inner voice, saying that I could not go back on my word and would not renege on my commitment.

My beliefs about money were what I had heard from people who up until then had taught and guided me. They always said, "Money is nothing; you can get money. When we die we won't take anything with us. Don't lose a friendship over money. Etc." The rest of the story is that I did not listen to my inner voice, or the external voice of my wife, I went through with the business, and lost my friend and the money.

I tripped up that time because I lacked wisdom in listening and perceiving that everything was not right and therefore the end results would not be right.

I have tried, based on my negative experiences, to listen to my inner voice. That voice does not err or fail; it is aware of everything that is happening and what is going to happen. The inner voice of a man is not the same as the voice of the mind.

I have said on different occasions that one of the faculties of the mind is to make us feel secure and for that reason, at the hour of making a decision, that voice speaks to us on the basis of fear in the unknown. The inner man is "God in us" and when we learn to listen to it we have divine power to make decisions. That inner voice is based on infinite wisdom instead of past experience or daily fears.

As yet I am not an expert on listening to my inner man and I have much to learn. We grow in this habit through the practice of prayer and meditation. It is in daily living and while we advance in this that the inner voice becomes more clear and evident.

When I wrote the book, *"More Than A Dream"*, by all appearances, it wasn't the best time for me to write a book. I didn't have the money to publish it, and I had no way of marketing it. If you have read any of my books you probably already know what I am talking about.

I had quite everything else I was doing and my perception of things, to start over again. But on that road I was disoriented, not knowing where to go. Without any income at the time, I was looking for ideas to generate the income that I needed. I had some experience in many things that I had done in my past, and I am one of those that believes that one carries money within oneself.

But I was disorientated, alone, and this affected my self-esteem to the point that my mind was fearful of considering as an option any ideas that I came up with or that were presented to me.

One day, God, who is within me, said to me that the way to go was to write a book. I started to write and it turned into a complete success, because He knew that not only could I write a book, but He would make sure to open the doors to market it. The good thing about listening to the inner man is that he doesn't indicate the way you should go to take you down the road of confusion, but rather to help you and take you to a higher level of living.

In Another Supernatural Dimension

There is another dimension that other beings of light control, and although we have access to it, we cannot operate in it entirely. In this dimension live the "... ministering spirits, sent to the service of those who will inherit salvation."

Men can see each other, but these beings cannot be seen easily. To be able to see them we have to enter their dimension through visions. I will quote some verses that talk about this, "In the year that King Uzziah died, I saw the Lord sitting on the throne, high and exalted, and the train of his robe filled the temple. Above Him were seraphs, each with six wings..." "Then one of the seraphs flew to me with a live coal in his hand..." Angels can be called, "flaming fires"; they are real and many people have seen them.

My wife was home alone with the children while I was speaking at a series of conferences en the State of Louisiana. Due to the fact that I was going to be visiting different places, I was to be out of town for more than 21 days.

One night, our younger girl, Melody, got sick and had a high fever. My wife had done everything she could to reduce the fever, but she could do nothing to bring it down. While sitting in the living room she told God: "I am sad. I feel that you have abandoned me!" The girl was sick, I was out of town, and she didn't know what to do to make our little girl better.

At that moment she looked out of the window and she saw a man looking at her. She immediately realized that he was from another dimension because he was taller than the height of the window and she was on the second floor of our house. The man must have been over 24 feet tall!

As my wife observed him a sense of trust came over her. The man leaned down, because he was taller than the height of the window, and asked, "What's the matter?" To which she replied, "I am sad, and I'm afraid, because my husband is not home and has been gone for many days and my daughter is very sick."

Then he said to her, "Don't be afraid because I am with you and you have never been nor ever will be, alone. Go and put the girl in bed."

My wife told me that she immediately felt a supernatural

peace and all anguish left her. She got up from the chair, signed the stranger to wait, and she went to put the little girl in bed, who she had been carrying in her arms all this time.

When she got to the bedroom the girl was calm, asleep and with no fever. She quickly put her girl down and went back to continue the conversation. But the giant was no longer there. You don't have to believe any of this, but my wife will bet her life she that is what she experienced. She knows that it was all real, and every time I watch her tell that story her eyes shine with enthusiasm and happiness.

On another occasion we were visiting a friend who had asked me to come to pray for him. He was quite sick. He couldn't stand up, or eat, or go to the bathroom, and his appearance was one who had returned from the grave.

We went together with our children, Wesser and Wesserline, who were quite young at the time. While we pronounced the blessing of God on him, the son came, who was about 2 years old, touching us and making sounds like he wanted to say something. We couldn't understand what he was trying to tell us and it took us awhile to figure out his baby-talk.

All of a sudden my wife and I turned to each other and said at the same time, "Wesserline!" We ran held on to the hand of the little boy and we found our daughter hanging by one hand from the balcony of the apartment. The son of my friend, who was more active than a monkey, had thrown our daughter over the railing and she was able to grab on to the balcony, hanging in thin air. I had to contort my body a thousand ways to reach her, grab her hand, and pull her up.

After the incident, my wife and I with our stomachs still in a knot, asked our friend how he felt. He said he no longer felt any pain or discomfort, and the color was coming back to his face, while ours was as pale as death itself. We left the house in a hurry with our two children. While we were going home my wife and I began to comment and talk about what had happened. "How was it possible for the little girl, who was barely old enough to walk, and wasn't even two years old yet, hang by one hand on the edge of the balcony and keep from falling onto some steel upright bars of construction on the ground level, which would have certainly killed her in an instant?" Where did our daughter get such strength to do such an incredible feat?

While we were talking, our little girl interrupted us, and

with her baby way of talking said, "an angel". Immediately, Sandra and I turned to her and said, "An angel? An angel, baby?" To which she replied that an angel had been with her.

One year later, when she had grown a bit more and could talk and explain things better, we asked her what had happened at the house of Julio Cesar, and she told us that while she was hanging and her fingers began to slip, and angel took her hands and held her there until we arrived and were able to rescue her from certain death.

About Medicine and Science

The light that illumines every man is above science and the light of men. On many occasions events or things happen that cannot be explained and that surpass the diagnostics of medics and psychologists. I myself have declared word of faith over people with cancer and it has disappeared, and this healing has been medically proven to be true.

One example of this was in New Jersey where I had been invited to a church to speak. I spoke, declared healing over those present, and later, the elder called me to come back because many sick had been healed, amongst whom were those sick with cancer.

When I went back, people came forward and testified that they had been healed, while others, who were afraid to believe that they had been healed, went to the doctor for a check up and the diagnosis was that they had truly been healed.

Then, in the Bronx I met a woman who had lost most of her family to cancer. She asked me to pray for her. I made a declaration of faith over her and she was healed of

> *The light that illumines every man is above science and the light of men.*

colon and intestinal cancer. For years this woman was one of the main collaborators of my ministry and to this woman was one of the main helpers in the ministers that I was developing, and to this day, she is healthy. These experiences I have seen in the lives of others and in my own, and that is why I can testify to the truth of what I am saying.

At the end of that year, due to the stress of the job, I was ill. I could hardly open my eyes, my whole head ached, and I could hardly get up. This made it hard for me to study, and though I had to begin my classes because I was in a boarding house, my grades were terrible. The university staff threatened to kick me out and the medication that the doctors prescribed for me did nothing.

One afternoon that I was very frustrated, I threw myself on my bed and there I opened my arms and looking up to God told Him that that was not how I wanted to live and if I could not study and live a normal life as the rest of the world, I would prefer to die. I said to Him with all seriousness, "Tomorrow I am well or dead." As yet I did not know the power of words, but I did know of the power of faith.

> *No one does anything significant without going through the setbacks of life. In fact, many times we fall from high positions to see ourselves in the midst of financial conflicts.*

That night I slept like a baby. It had been a long time since I had slept like that. The next day when I woke up I was alive, and of course, healed. Since then, all of those complications of my head disappeared and I now live a normal life.

While I worked at selling books so I could continue my studies, I developed a serious problem in my stomach. I didn't pay much attention to it though, because I thought it was stress related. I ate bread and drank milk to mitigate the pain.

I returned to the university boarding house at the

beginning of classes and throughout the whole year the pains in my stomach only got worse. One day I felt like vomiting and what came out was raw blood. Then I realized I had a serious problem. I went to the doctor and he diagnosed me with ulcers, game me some medication, but the problem didn't get any better.

One day when I was in my room, I felt the desire to ask God for help regarding my problem and even though I always did that, that day was different because my inner man was active and speaking to me clearly. So I declared the favor of the Almighty over my illness and before getting up off my knees a soft voice spoke to me, "Never again will you suffer from your stomach."

After that the pain and discomfort disappeared and every time I feel any discomfort of any kind, I speak to the stomach and tell it that God healed me and it no longer has permission to be sick ever again.

About Finances and Needs

No one does anything significant without going through the setbacks of life. In fact, many times we fall from high positions to see ourselves in the midst of financial conflicts. King David said, "They that wait upon the

Eternal One will be like a tree planted by streams of water, which yields its fruit in season and whose leaf does not wither. Whatever he does will prosper."

Money is one of the tools that the Infinite One has provided for His children to be happy. But the reality is, not everyone is financially stable as they wish they were, either because something went wrong, or because they are starting a new project, or due to bankruptcy.

I remember that I was starting a new congregation the Bronx, New York, and I had no money. I had just arrived to this country and the Association under which I was working was putting things in order. My salary was delayed and after two months I had no way of paying my rent. Under those circumstances, I asked God to do something miraculous.

One day the director of Evangelism called me and said that a woman, who was previously a member of one of the churches belonging to the Association and had left due to some serious problems with her son, had asked that I call her.

So I did, and as we talked she began to tell me about her son's situation and how he had gotten into drugs and how everyone had abandoned her, leaving her to struggle by herself to deal with this problem.

I told her that I was going to declare the love of God over her son and do matter where he was something supernatural would happen to him. She said her son was not with her; he was in school. I replied that it didn't matter. The words that I would declare over him would be carried by supernatural means and a miracle would happen.

So I did. I declared the favor and goodness of God over her and her son. I remember I said something like, "Wherever your son is at this time, something supernatural will happen to him so he realizes he is not along in this problem and that God loves him."

We ended our conversation and the next weekend, while I was saying good-bye to the people, this woman came up to me and gave me an envelope. I thought she was giving me a list of prayer requests. I greeted her, smiled, and put the envelope in the inside pocket of my suit coat jacket.

Two days later I received a call from the woman. She said, "Last Saturday I didn't tell you what happened to my son because I saw you were busy greeting the people.

When my son came home from school that day, he said something strange had happened to him. He was leaving the school to do drugs and while he was on his way out something strange diverted him to a side room and made him sit in a chair." And then she added enthusiastically, "When my son got home from school he asked me if I had prayed for him at that time. I said I had and that the pastor had called and I had asked him to pray for him." He said, "Well, it must have been God that was with me then."

We finished talking and she had finished telling me her exciting news, instead of being happy, I was sad, because I could only think of how come God could use me to channel His power but I don't have enough to pay my rent. With that thought on my mind I went to my room and began to wrestle with God. I told Him what I was thinking and how I felt and I began to recite some verses from memory of the promises that He had given men in ancient times.

Then I heard the Spirit (the light) telling me, "Remember the envelope that Maria (her real name is changed) gave you?" "Yes," I answered. "But now is not a good time to pray for Maria, besides, her major problem is solved, that is with her son, and the rest can wait."

In the midst of the conversation with the inner Light, I got up, and reluctantly went looking for the envelope. When I opened it I saw dollars. My first reaction was, well ok a few dollars, but I began checking the size of the bills and I began to count them. $100, $200, $300, $400, $500, $600, $700, $800, $900, $1,000 dollars! What I needed for the rent was only $600 and the envelope had $1,000.

Everything in life is that way. God has provided for every one of His children more than they need. But because of our unbelief we have kept it in an envelope and we don't use it. People live in want, while the universe holds an abundance for all. It is not for certain few, or for a special group, "because the true Light that gives light to the world was coming to this world." I don't just say that it illumines every man, but takes care of, provides for, heals, blesses and prospers every man.

I conclude by saying that I firmly believe that a man's thoughts have power over him. "For as he thinks in his heart, so is he." Words are a divine entity and a power that activates the supernatural in order for this to be converted into something natural and visible.

I also know that faith is what makes the unseen be seen, causing things to flow in the natural. But above all these powers that have been given to man, there is a superior power yet. There is a greater light than all others. This is what keeps our light on and makes things happen.

God does not always use the method of miracles, because He wants us to grow through our own decisions, and that we use the powers that He has already given us, and that are part of our being, such as words, decisions, thoughts, actions, and above all, the power to strive and develop all the good qualities that we have inside of us.

When you feel that no one hears you, that everything is going wrong, and you failed, you can be sure that if you ask Him, He will do it. Many people take the misfortunes of life as a proof that God doesn't exists, when in reality, this is way in which the Eternal tells us, "I love you so much, but I don't want to interfere in your world and in your desires. I want you to make your own decisions, develop your qualities, and find out that all my power is within you, and the only thing you need is to accept it and take it.

But remember that if you need help, I am here. When you're tired, you can count on me. And when something seems impossible to you: "Call me and I will answer you and tell you great and unsearchable things you don't know."

How many doors have opened to me in a miraculous way by declaring a word of wisdom or knowledge over a leader. I, of all people, realize that the power is not natural, that it is supernatural within me, it opens my heart, and becomes my friend and helps me to go places and receive blessings that I otherwise would not have achieved.

The Power of Light

Notes

- Wikipedia, The Free Encyclopedia, www.wikipedia.org
- Genesis 1
- Mark 9:23
- Proverbs 23:7
- Luke 6:45
- Matthew 17:20
- John 20:21-22
- John 1:9-11
- John 6:63
- Hebrews 11:6
- Wikipedia, The Free Encyclopedia, www.wikipedia.org
- Genesis 2:7
- John 6:63
- Matthew 15:19
- Hebrews 4:12
- John 13:17
- John 14:12
- Genesis 3:6
- Romans 12:1-2
- Ephesians 4:23
- Matthew 15:1, 15
- Matthew 15:16; 6:18; 6:22
- Matthew 8:14, 15
- Galatians 3:26; 4:6

- Romans 8:17
- Romans 3:16; 6:19; 6:17; 12:27
- Ephesians 5:3; 5:17 5:18-19; 1:12; 3:26, 28
- Genesis 1:1
- 1 Corinthians 1:2
- Philippians 1:1
- Colossians 1:2
- Ephesians 2:10; 2:19; 3:1; 4:1; 4:24; 3:20
- Ephesians 2:6; 3:3; 3:4; 3:12
- 1 Thessalonians 1:4
- 1 Thessalonians 5:5; 3:1; 3:14; 2:5; 2:9-10; 2:11; 5:8; 3:1-2; 5:18